OPPOSING
VIEWPOINTS®
SERIES

I Atheism

Other Books of Related Interest:

Opposing Viewpoints Series

American Values

At Issue Series

White Supremacy Groups

Current Controversies Series

Censorship

"Congress shall make no law . . . abridging the freedom of speech, or of the press."

First Amendment to the U.S. Constitution

The basic foundation of our democracy is the First Amendment guarantee of freedom of expression. The Opposing Viewpoints Series is dedicated to the concept of this basic freedom and the idea that it is more important to practice it than to enshrine it.

OPPOSING
VIEWPOINTS®
SERIES

Atheism

Beth Rosenthal, Book Editor

GREENHAVEN PRESS
A part of Gale, Cengage Learning

GALE
CENGAGE Learning™

Detroit • New York • San Francisco • New Haven, Conn • Waterville, Maine • London

GALE
CENGAGE Learning™

Christine Nasso, *Publisher*
Elizabeth Des Chenes, *Managing Editor*

© 2009 Greenhaven Press, a part of Gale, Cengage Learning.

Gale and Greenhaven Press are registered trademarks used herein under license.

For more information, contact:
Greenhaven Press
27500 Drake Rd.
Farmington Hills, MI 48331-3535
Or you can visit our Internet site at gale.cengage.com

For product information and technology assistance, contact us at

Gale Customer Support, 1-800-877-4253
For permission to use material from this text or product, submit all requests online at www.cengage.com/permissions

Further permissions questions can be emailed to permissionrequest@cengage.com

Articles in Greenhaven Press anthologies are often edited for length to meet page require- ments. In addition, original titles of these works are changed to clearly present the main thesis and to explicitly indicate the author's opinion. Every effort is made to ensure that Greenhaven Press accurately reflects the original intent of the authors. Every effort has been made to trace the owners of copyrighted material.

Cover photograph reproduced by © Ccaetano/Dreamstime.com.

LIBRARY OF CONGRESS CATALOGING-IN-PUBLICATION DATA

Atheism / Beth Rosenthal, book editor.
  p. cm. -- (Opposing viewpoints)
  Includes bibliographical references and index.
  ISBN 978-0-7377-4192-6 (hardcover)
  ISBN 978-0-7377-4193-3 (pbk.)
  1. Atheism. I. Rosenthal, Beth, 1964-
  BL2747.3.A796 2009
  211'.8--dc22
                                                    2008051453

Printed in the United States of America
1 2 3 4 5 6 7 13 12 11 10 09

Contents

Why Consider Opposing Viewpoints?

> *"The only way in which a human being can make some approach to knowing the whole of a subject is by hearing what can be said about it by persons of every variety of opinion and studying all modes in which it can be looked at by every character of mind. No wise man ever acquired his wisdom in any mode but this."*
>
> *John Stuart Mill*

In our media-intensive culture it is not difficult to find differing opinions. Thousands of newspapers and magazines and dozens of radio and television talk shows resound with differing points of view. The difficulty lies in deciding which opinion to agree with and which "experts" seem the most credible. The more inundated we become with differing opinions and claims, the more essential it is to hone critical reading and thinking skills to evaluate these ideas. Opposing Viewpoints books address this problem directly by presenting stimulating debates that can be used to enhance and teach these skills. The varied opinions contained in each book examine many different aspects of a single issue. While examining these conveniently edited opposing views, readers can develop critical thinking skills such as the ability to compare and contrast authors' credibility, facts, argumentation styles, use of persuasive techniques, and other stylistic tools. In short, the Opposing Viewpoints Series is an ideal way to attain the higher-level thinking and reading skills so essential in a culture of diverse and contradictory opinions.

In addition to providing a tool for critical thinking, Opposing Viewpoints books challenge readers to question their own strongly held opinions and assumptions. Most people form their opinions on the basis of upbringing, peer pressure, and personal, cultural, or professional bias. By reading carefully balanced opposing views, readers must directly confront new ideas as well as the opinions of those with whom they disagree. This is not to simplistically argue that everyone who reads opposing views will—or should—change his or her opinion. Instead, the series enhances readers' understanding of their own views by encouraging confrontation with opposing ideas. Careful examination of others' views can lead to the readers' understanding of the logical inconsistencies in their own opinions, perspective on why they hold an opinion, and the consideration of the possibility that their opinion requires further evaluation.

Evaluating Other Opinions

To ensure that this type of examination occurs, Opposing Viewpoints books present all types of opinions. Prominent spokespeople on different sides of each issue as well as well-known professionals from many disciplines challenge the reader. An additional goal of the series is to provide a forum for other, less known, or even unpopular viewpoints. The opinion of an ordinary person who has had to make the decision to cut off life support from a terminally ill relative, for example, may be just as valuable and provide just as much insight as a medical ethicist's professional opinion. The editors have two additional purposes in including these less known views. One, the editors encourage readers to respect others' opinions—even when not enhanced by professional credibility. It is only by reading or listening to and objectively evaluating others' ideas that one can determine whether they are worthy of consideration. Two, the inclusion of such viewpoints encourages the important critical thinking skill of objectively evaluating an author's credentials and bias. This evaluation will illuminate an author's reasons for taking a particular stance on an issue and will aid in readers' evaluation of the author's ideas.

It is our hope that these books will give readers a deeper understanding of the issues debated and an appreciation of the complexity of even seemingly simple issues when good and honest people disagree. This awareness is particularly important in a democratic society such as ours in which people enter into public debate to determine the common good. Those with whom one disagrees should not be regarded as enemies but rather as people whose views deserve careful examination and may shed light on one's own.

Thomas Jefferson once said that "difference of opinion leads to inquiry, and inquiry to truth." Jefferson, a broadly educated man, argued that "if a nation expects to be ignorant and free ... it expects what never was and never will be." As individuals and as a nation, it is imperative that we consider the opinions of others and examine them with skill and discernment. The Opposing Viewpoints Series is intended to help readers achieve this goal.

David L. Bender and Bruno Leone,
Founders

Introduction

> *"Congress shall make no law respecting an establishment of religion, or prohibiting the free exercise thereof; or abridging the freedom of speech, or of the press; or the right of the people peaceably to assemble, and to petition the Government for a redress of grievances."*
>
> —First Amendment of
> the U.S. Constitution

Throughout history, there has been an enormous amount of distrust and tension between those who believe in God and those who don't. The religious maintain that God and organized religion serve as a moral compass for society, while atheists contend that belief in a god or gods, as well as the institutions of organized religions, is not necessary to living a moral life. The friction between atheists and the religious faithful has been apparent in numerous debates, such as whether creationism should be taught alongside evolution in school and whether the Pledge of Allegiance should include the phrase "under God."

The phrase "under God" was added to the Pledge of Allegiance in 1954, a time when it was still legal in the United States for public schools to mandate Bible study as part of the curriculum. But the nation was on the verge of dramatic change. Over the next decade or so, the civil rights movement redefined race relations, the Vietnam War became the catalyst for many protest movements worldwide, and many Americans, particularly young people, found themselves questioning the nation's institutions, including organized religion. Writes John W. Whitehead of the Rutherford Institute, "By 1963, the time was not only ripe for change in the public schools but the nation as well. America was on the cusp of a bevy of movements that were to literally change the face of the country. The Protestant ethic that had once determined American values and ruled in public education was one of the first to crumble. Moreover, forced prayer and Bible reading clearly alienated the Jews and other minority religions. Thus, these practices were doomed in a generation of young people who were throwing off the shackles of the establishment—including the church."

It was against this backdrop that landmark battles were fought in the Supreme Court over the issue of religion in schools. It was the Court's decision in *Engel v. Vitale* in 1962 that effectively put a stop to organized prayer in school by finding that such prayer violated the ban on government-sponsored religion. However, many people associate the end of school prayer with *Murray v. Curlett*, which was decided by the Supreme Court in 1963. The case challenged a Baltimore, Maryland, statute that required that the Lord's Prayer or the Bible be read in public school classes. Decided jointly with *Abington School District v. Schempp*, which challenged a Pennsylvania law that public school students must read 10 Bible verses each day, the Court found that both cases infringed on the religious freedom of children as established by the free exercise clause and the establishment clause of the First Amendment. *Murray v. Curlett* had particular significance for atheists. According to the American Atheists' Web site, "The *Murray v. Curlett* case was actually the first of its kind—it addressed not just the question of 'religious liberty' for believers, but the notion of liberties for atheists."

Before *Engle v. Vitale*, *Murray v. Curlett*, and *Abington School District v. Schempp* were decided, students in the United States read from the Bible and prayed in public school classes daily. For many religious believers, the legal decisions banning prayer and Bible study in school only strengthened their fears that religion was being replaced by a system of thought that undermined the nation's most cherished values.

The *Murray v. Curlett* case was brought by Madalyn Murray O'Hair, a prominent atheist whose profile was raised considerably after the Court's decision. O'Hair, who founded American Atheists in 1963, was revered by many, but not all, of her fellow atheists and was demonized by the religious. She was a controversial figure not only because of her vocal support for atheism, but also because many felt she was intolerant and dismissive of those who disagreed with her. O'Hair was seen as the voice of the atheist movement, and many felt that the atheist movement suffered by association. As Bill Cook notes in an article for *Free Inquiry*, "The O'Hairs frequently referred to themselves in their own literature as the First Family of Atheism, all suitably capitalized. More specifically, O'Hair described herself as the best-educated, most widely known atheist leader in the United States. Elsewhere, she described herself not simply as an atheist, but as *the* atheist. . . . The problem lies in the way they [the O'Hairs] encouraged much of this hostility by their own actions, and so tarnished the wider atheist cause."

While supporters of O'Hair acknowledge her faults, they stress that she helped to give purpose to a movement when it needed it. They believe her contributions must be viewed within the context of the 1950s and 1960s, with the civil rights and women's movements taking hold. Conrad F. Goeringer explains at the American Atheists' Web site: "She 'desensitized' the American cultural landscape, at least to the extent that atheists today are not quite so driven into that dark closet of marginalization and timidity as they were in the 1950s or 1960s. She also raised important philosophical issues in an activist context during a tumultuous period in American history. Her challenges to god belief and government sponsorship of religion came at a time when Americans were reexamining—often painfully—other sacred artifacts of their culture."

By the start of the twenty-first century, a new crop of atheist thinkers had achieved prominence—and sparked renewed controversy—on the world stage. Sometimes referred to as "new atheists," this group includes Richard Dawkins, Sam Harris, and Daniel C. Dennett. The new atheists have drawn the admiration of millions worldwide; supporters praise their articulate defense of their philosophy. These thinkers have been criticized, however, for what many see as their condescending and patronizing attitude toward religion. In a January 5, 2007, *Wall Street Journal* article, Sam Schulman writes, "For the new atheists, believing in God is a form of stupidity, which sets off their own intelligence. . . . They argue as if these questions are easily answered by their own blunt materialism. Most of all, they assume that no intelligent, reflective person could ever defend religion rather than dismiss it."

As it has for hundreds of years, the subject of atheism continues to prompt impassioned debate. Many facets of this debate are examined in *Opposing Viewpoints: Atheism*, with chapters that explore the following questions: What Is the State of Atheism? What Is Atheism's Impact on Society? What Are the Major Concerns of Atheism? and What Is the Future of Atheism? The viewpoints presented in this volume examine this provocative subject that offers reason and solace to some, while causing alarm and distrust in others.

OPPOSING
VIEWPOINTS®
SERIES

CHAPTER 1

What Is the State of Atheism?

Chapter Preface

In recent decades, there has been much debate over the issue of school vouchers. A school voucher gives parents the option of sending their children to a private school if they are unhappy with their public school. According to the Education Bug Web site, "School voucher programs allow parents to use monetary vouchers from the city, state or federal government to pay for their children's private school education." Depending on the kind of voucher program, vouchers can be applied by students to go to any school, or are only given to lower-income students or to those students who go to schools that fail to meet general standard requirements. A voucher is usually equal to the amount that is spent by a public school on each of its students.

Many atheists take issue with the idea of school vouchers, arguing that allowing some families to use government funds to send their children to private schools, including religious schools, means that taxpayers are being forced to make involuntary contributions to religious groups. The Americans United for Separation of Church and State explains this position: "Often, religious schools promote sectarian dogma and take controversial stands on issues such as gay rights, the role of women in society and reproductive freedom. Taxpayers should not be required to subsidize the spread of religious/moral opinions they may strongly disagree with. All religious projects including schooling should be funded with voluntary contributions from church members."

Supporters of school vouchers point to the need to give parents the final choice in deciding on the school that will provide the best education for their children. They contend that parents' desire to give their children the best possible education should not be undermined by efforts to maintain the separation between religion and government. These advocates reason that a ban on vouchers would do far more harm than good, asserting that low-income students in struggling school districts—some of whom might want to use vouchers to go to religious schools—would have to remain in second-rate schools. In an article for the *Jewish World Review*, Suzanne Fields argues that "How vouchers are used depends on a family's choice, not a bureaucrat's whim, and it's silly to argue that vouchers break down the wall between church and state. Does a state-subsidized senior who chooses a church-affiliated nursing home breach that wall? Vouchers are not about establishing a state-based religion, but empowering parents of moderate means to educate their children as they choose—just like parents who can afford private schools."

The authors in this chapter debate the state of atheism in society, discussing the prevalence of atheism, different views on the existence of God, and whether or not children should be raised with religion. As the debate over vouchers illustrates, the state of atheism today is tied to an ongoing struggle to balance the rights and beliefs of the religious and the nonreligious.

> *"Get your act together, folks—your seismic detection systems, your first responders and global mobilization capacity—because no one, and I do mean no One—is coming to medi-vac us out of here."*

Atheists Question God's Existence

Barbara Ehrenreich

In the following viewpoint, Barbara Ehrenreich contends that people who believe in God should question their belief after the devastation of the tsunami that took place on December 26, 2004. Questioning whether God actually exists, she argues that a kind and compassionate God would not allow wars or catastrophic events to happen. Ehrenreich, a columnist for The Progressive, *is the author of* Nickel and Dimed: On (Not) Getting By in America *and* Blood Rites: Origins and History of the Passions of War.

As you read, consider the following questions:

 1. According to the author, what is "theodicy"?

Barbara Ehrenreich, "God Owes Us an Apology," *The Progressive*, vol. 69, March 2005, p. 16. Copyright © 2005 by The Progressive, Inc. Reproduced by permission of The Progressive, 409 East Main Street, Madison, WI 53703, www.progressive.org.16.

2. In Ehrenreich's opinion, why should people question their belief in God after an incident such as a tsunami?

3. According to the author, when did the concept of a benevolent and strong God emerge?

The tsunami of sea water [in December 2004] was followed instantly by a tsunami of spittle as the religious sputtered to rationalize God's latest felony. Here we'd been placidly killing each other a few dozen at a time in Iraq, Darfur, Congo, Israel, and Palestine, when along comes the deity and whacks a quarter million in a couple of hours between breakfast and lunch. On CNN, NPR, Fox News, and in newspaper articles too numerous for Nexis to count, men and women of the cloth weighed in solemnly on His existence, His motives, and even His competence to continue as Ruler of Everything.

Where Is God When You Need Him?

Theodicy, in other words—the attempt to reconcile God's perfect goodness with the manifest evils of His world—has arisen from the waves. On the retro, fundamentalist, side, various men of the cloth announced that the tsunami was the rational act of a deity enraged by (take your pick): the suppression of Christianity in South Asia, pornography and child-trafficking in that same locale, or, in the view of some Muslim commentators, the bikini-clad tourists at Phuket.

On the more liberal end of the theological spectrum, God's spokespeople hastened to stuff their fingers in the dike even as the floodwaters of doubt washed over it. Of course, God exists, seems to be the general consensus. And, of course, He is perfectly good. It's just that his jurisdiction doesn't extend to tectonic plates. Or maybe it does and He tosses us an occasional grenade like this just to see how quickly we can mobilize to clean up the damage. Besides, as the Catholic priests like to remind us, "He's a 'mystery'"—though that's never stopped them from pronouncing His views on abortion with absolute certainty.

There Is No Proof of God's Existence

Who is this "God" in whose name so many diverse and troubling things take place? Why is it assumed to be good to affirm one's faith in such an entity? Why is it thought to be wicked to deny its existence? Most striking about so much talk of "God," both to affirm and to deny, is the way in which many who use this language seem to know exactly to what and/or whom it refers.

James Carroll, "All God, All the Time,"
Boston Globe, *October 17, 2005, p. A15.*

The clerics who are struggling to make sense of the tsunami must not have noticed that this is hardly the first display of God's penchant for wanton, homicidal mischief. Leaving out man-made genocide, war, and even those "natural" disasters, like drought and famine, to which "man" invariably contributes through his inept social arrangements, God has a lot to account for in the way of earthquakes, hurricanes, tornadoes, and plagues. Nor has He ever shown much discrimination in his choice of victims. A tsunami hit Lisbon in 1755, on All Saints Day, when the good Christians were all in church. The faithful perished, while the denizens of the red light district, which was built on strong stone, simply carried on sinning. Similarly, last fall's [2004] hurricanes flattened the God-fearing, Republican parts of Florida while sparing sin-soaked Key West and South Beach.

The Christian-style "God of love" should be particularly vulnerable to post-tsunami doubts. What kind of "love" inspired Him to wrest babies from their parents' arms, the better to drown them in a hurry? If He so loves us that He gave his only son etc., why couldn't he have held those tectonic plates in place at least until the kids were off the beach? So much, too, for the current pop-Christian God, who can be found, at least on the Internet, micro-managing people's careers, resolving marital spats, and taking excess pounds off the faithful—his last being Pat Robertson's latest fixation.

We Need to Question Our Belief in God

If we are responsible for our actions, as most religions insist, then God should be, too, and I would propose, post-tsunami, an immediate withdrawal of prayer and other forms of flattery directed at a supposedly moral deity—at least until an apology is issued, such as, for example: "I was so busy with Cindy-in-Omaha's weight-loss program that I wasn't paying attention to the Earth's crust."

It's not just Christianity. Any religion centered on a God who is both all-powerful and all-good, including Islam and the more monotheistically inclined versions of Hinduism, should be subject to a thorough post-tsunami evaluation. As many have noted before me: If God cares about our puny species, then disasters prove that he is not all-powerful; and if he is all-powerful, then clearly he doesn't give a damn.

In fact, the best way for the religious to fend off the atheist threat might be to revive the old bad—or at least amoral and indifferent—gods. The tortured notion of a God who is both good and powerful is fairly recent, dating to roughly 1200 BC, after which Judaism, Christianity, Buddhism, and Islam emerged. Before that, you had the feckless Greco-Roman pantheon, whose members interfered in human events only when their considerable egos were at stake. Or you had monstrous, human-sacrifice-consuming, psychogods like Ba al and his Central American counterparts. Even earlier, as I pointed out in my book *Blood Rites*, there were prehistoric god(desses) modeled on man-eating animals like lions, and requiring a steady diet of human or animal sacrificial flesh.

The faithful will protest that they don't want to worship a bad—or amoral or indifferent—God, but obviously they already do. Why not acknowledge what our prehistoric ancestors knew? If the Big Guy or Gal operates in any kind of moral framework, it has nothing to do with the rules we've come up with over the eons as primates attempting to live in groups—rules like, for example, "no hitting."

Don't Rely on God—If There Is One—to Help

Yes, 12/26 [2004] was a warning, though not about the hazards of wearing bikinis. What it comes down to is that we're up shit creek here on the planet Earth. We're wide open to asteroid hits, with the latest near-miss coming in October [2004], when a city-sized one passed within a mere million miles of Earth, which is just four times the distance between the Earth and the moon. Then, too, it's only a matter of time before the constant shuffling of viral DNA results in a global pandemic. And 12/26 was a reminder that the planet itself is a jerry-rigged affair, likely to keep belching and lurching. Even leaving out global warming and the possibility of nuclear war, this is not a good situation, in case you hadn't noticed so far.

If there is a God, and He, She, or It had a message for us on 12/26, that message is: Get your act together, folks—your seismic detection systems, your first responders and global mobilization capacity—because no one, and I do mean no One, is coming to medi-vac us out of here.

VIEWPOINT *2*

> *"Religions survive and flourish because they are a call to membership—they provide customs, beliefs and rituals that unite the generations in a shared way of life, and implant the seeds of mutual respect."*

Western Religions Accept God's Existence

Roger Scruton

In the following viewpoint, Roger Scruton argues that there is nothing irrational about believing that God exists because prayer and faith help us to find answers to our questions about life. He maintains that wars fought over land have happened when countries, such as Nazi Germany, have removed religion from society. Scruton is a research professor at the Institute for the Psychological Sciences in Arlington, Virginia, and a visiting scholar at Oxford University.

As you read, consider the following questions:

1. According to Roger Scruton, what is a religious meme?

2. In Scruton's opinion, how do religions reveal their meaning?

Roger Scruton, "Why Dawkins Is Wrong About God," *The Spectator*, January 14, 2006, p. 24. Copyright © 2006 by *The Spectator*. Reproduced by permission of *The Spectator*.

3. In Richard Dawkins's opinion, what is the purpose of religious mysteries, according to the author?

Faced with the spectacle of the cruelties perpetrated in the name of faith, Voltaire [a French philosopher who defended the right to freedom of religion] famously cried 'Ecrasez l'infame' ["crush the infamy"]. Scores of enlightened thinkers have followed him, declaring organized religion to be the enemy of mankind, the force that divides the believer from the infidel and thereby both excites and authorises murder. Richard Dawkins, whose TV series *The Root of All Evil?* concludes [in 2006], is the most influential living example of this tradition. And he has embellished it with a striking theory of his own—the theory of the religious 'meme'. A meme is a mental entity that colonises the brains of people, much as a virus colonises a cell. The meme exploits its host in order to reproduce itself, spreading from brain to brain like meningitis, and killing off the competing powers of rational argument. Like genes and species, memes are Darwinian individuals, whose success or failure depends upon their ability to find the ecological niche that enables reproduction. Such is the nature of 'gerin oil', as Dawkins contemptuously describes religion.

This analogical extension of the theory of biological reproduction has a startling quality. It seems to explain the extraordinary survival power of nonsense, and the constant 'sleep of reason' that, in [Spanish painter Francisco] Goya's engraving, 'calls forth monsters'. Faced with a page of [French philosopher Jacques] Derrida and knowing that this drivel is being read and reproduced in a thousand American campuses, I have often found myself tempted by the theory of the meme. The page in my hand is clearly the product of a diseased brain, and the disease is massively infectious: Derrida admitted as much when he referred to the Meconstructive virus.

All the same, I am not entirely persuaded by this extension by analogy of genetics. The theory that ideas have a disposition to propagate themselves by appropriating energy from the brains that harbour them recalls [French playwright] Moliere's medical expert who explained the fact that opium induces sleep by referring to its virtus dopmitiva (the ability to cause sleep). It only begins to look like an explanation when we read back into the alleged cause the distinguishing features of the effect, by imagining ideas as entities whose existence depends, as genes and species do, on reproduction.

Nevertheless, let us grant Dawkins his stab at a theory. We should still remember that not every dependent organism destroys its host. In addition to parasites there are symbionts and mutualists—invaders that either do not impede or positively amplify their host's reproductive chances. And which is religion? Why has religion survived, if it has conferred no benefit on its adepts? And what happens to societies that have been vaccinated against the infection—Soviet society, for instance, or Nazi Germany—do they experience a gain in reproductive potential? Clearly, a lot more research is needed if we are to come down firmly on the side of mass vaccination rather than (my preferred option) lending support to the religion that seems most suited to temper our belligerent instincts, and which, in doing so, asks us to forgive those who trespass against us and humbly atone for our faults.

So there are bad memes and good memes. Consider mathematics. This propagates itself through human brains because it is true; people entirely without maths—who cannot count, subtract or multiply—don't have children, for the simple reason that they make fatal mistakes before they get there. Maths is a real mutualist. Of course the same is not true of bad maths; but bad maths doesn't survive, precisely because it destroys the brains in which it takes up residence.

Religion's Mysteries Can Be Found Through Prayer and Belief

Maybe religion is to this extent like maths: that its survival has something to do with its truth. Of course, it is not the lit-

There Is No Purpose Without God

We long for love, harmony and sympathy because we are intended by a Creator to find them. In a world without God, however, this desire for love and purpose is a cruel joke of nature—imprinted by evolution, but destined for disappointment, just as we are destined for oblivion, on a planet that will be consumed by fire before the sun grows dim and cold.

Michael Gerson,
"What Atheists Can't Answer,"
Washington Post, *July 13, 2007, p. A17.*

eral truth, nor the whole truth. Indeed, the truth of a religion lies less in what is revealed in its doctrines than in what is concealed in its mysteries. Religions do not reveal their meaning directly because they cannot do so; their meaning has to be earned by worship and prayer, and by a life of quiet obedience. Nevertheless, truths that are hidden are still truths; and maybe we can be guided by them only if they are hidden, just as we are guided by the sun only if we do not look at it. The direct encounter with religious truth would be like Semele's encounter with Zeus, a sudden conflagration.

To Dawkins that idea of a purely religious truth is hogwash. The mysteries of religion, he will say, exist in order to forbid all questioning, so giving religion the edge over science in the struggle for survival. In any case, why are there so many competitors among religions, if they are competing for the truth? Shouldn't the false ones have fallen by the wayside, like refuted theories in science? And how does religion improve the human spirit, when it seems to authorise the crimes now committed each day by Islamists, and which are in turn no more than a shadow of the crimes that were spread across Europe by the Thirty Years War [1618–1648]?

Christianity Is a Peacekeeper

Those are big questions, not to be solved by a TV programme, so here in outline are my answers. Religions survive and flourish because they are a call to membership—they provide customs, beliefs and rituals that unite the generations in a shared way of life, and implant the seeds of mutual respect. Like every form of social life, they are inflamed at the edges, where they compete for territory with other faiths. To blame religion for the wars conducted in its name, however, is like blaming love for the Trojan War. All human motives, even the most noble, will feed the flames of conflict when subsumed by the 'territorial imperative—this, too, Darwin teaches us, and Dawkins surely must have noticed it. Take religion away, as the Nazis and the Communists did, and you do nothing to suppress the pursuit of Lebensraum ["living space"]. You simply remove the principal source of mercy in the ordinary human heart and so make war pitiless; atheism found its proof at Stalingrad.

There is a tendency, fed by the sensationalism of television, to judge all human institutions by their behaviour in times of conflict. Religion, like patriotism, gets a bad press among those for whom war is the one human reality, the one occasion when the Other in all of us is noticeable. But the real test of a human institution is in peacetime. Peace is boring, quotidian [ordinary], and also rotten television. But you can learn about it from books. Those nurtured in the Christian faith know that Christianity's ability to maintain peace in the world around us reflects its gift of peace to the world within. In a Christian society there is no need for Asbos [Anti-Social Behaviour Orders, given as civil orders in the United Kingdom and Ireland], and in the world after religion those Asbos will do no good—they are a last desperate attempt to save us from the effects of godlessness, and the attempt is doomed.

Religion Is the Search for Love and Acceptance

Muslims say similar things, and so do Jews. So who possesses the truth, and how would you know? Well, we don't know, nor do we need to know. All faith depends on revelation, and the proof of the revelation is in the peace that it brings. Rational argument can get us just so far, in raising the monotheistic faiths above the muddled world of superstition. It can help us to understand the real difference between a faith that commands us to forgive our enemies, and one that commands us to slaughter them. But the leap of faith itself—this placing of your life at God's service—is a leap over reason's edge. This does not make it irrational, any more than falling in love is irrational. On the contrary, it is the heart's submission to an ideal, and a bid for the love, peace and forgiveness that Dawkins too is seeking, since he, like the rest of us, was made in just that way.

> *"I am urging parents to expose their children to the many other ways, including the way I have chosen: no religion at all."*

Children Should Be Raised with an Awareness of Atheism

Nica Lalli

In the following viewpoint, Nica Lalli maintains that it is important to teach children to question life and that a parent's religious beliefs limit that ability. She contends that a child who is taught to follow specific religious beliefs does not learn how to make her own choices about religion and God. Lalli, a writer and teacher in Brooklyn, New York, is the author of Nothing: Something to Believe In.

As you read, consider the following questions:

1. According to Nica Lalli, are her children atheists?
2. In Lalli's opinion, can a child of religious parents truly question religious beliefs?

3. As Lalli asserts, why should good parenting have no religious affiliation?

I am an atheist. I have never joined, or been part of, any religious group or organization. I was raised without religion, and without much understanding of what religion is. I have never had much of an identity religiously, and I stayed away from much thought or discussion on the matter. It is only recently that I have really explored the many options for religious beliefs and have decided that rather than saying, "No comment," I now call myself an atheist.

I am also a parent. I have two children: a 13-year-old daughter and a 10-year-old son. They don't belong to any religious group, either. I never had them baptized, christened, or blessed. Neither of them had a bris, bat mitzvah or first communion. But am I raising "atheist children"? Just because I do not identify our family as religious, are they atheists? I don't think so. Rather, I am raising questioning children, and those are the best kind of children to send out into the world.

Religion Does Not Leave Room for Questions

I never describe our family as "an atheist family" (I prefer to say, "We are nothing," as in not part of any religion), and I reject the notion that my kids are automatically what I am. I think that keeping them open to all the possibilities is more important than telling them what to believe in.

I know a lot of religious families who say they are a Christian, Jewish or Muslim family. And they are. They have traditions, rituals and celebrations that define what they are. They pass those things to the children, along with belief.

Most young children accept what their parents tell them as true, whether it is the existence of Santa Claus or Jesus Christ. It is important that children understand what their parents believe, but it is also important for children to know about all

Expose Your Children to Many Different Religions

Exclusive exposure to a single religion leads to ignorant, blinkered thinking, but exposure to multiple religions reveals religion as a human cultural artifact and denies any one of them the high ground.

The study of religion—as opposed to indoctrination *into* religion—aids our understanding of the religiously saturated world around us. It can also inoculate our kids against the more poisonous religious ideas.

Dale McGowan, "Tossing the Round Peg: The Power and Joy of Secular Parenting," Secular Nation, *July 2007, p. 12.*

the options out there. This is tricky if a parent is a true believer of a religion and feels that her way is the only path. But how can children question openly when they are taught that there are absolute truths in belief?

Teach Your Kids to Think for Themselves

In the past few years, my kids have really started to ask tough questions about the world and how our ideas fit into it. I have to admit that I don't have all the answers.

We struggle together to understand what it all means. I teach them about all the major religions, and when I am not sure, I call friends who are part of the religions in question for better answers. We look at the art made to honor deities, we read stories written to explain belief systems, and we talk about similarities and differences among religions, both extinct and still in existence today. I try to keep all the possibilities open to them, and I answer all their questions honestly. I admit that I do not believe in the many gods that are out there, but I respect people who choose to follow them.

I may be raising my kids outside organized religion, but I am not raising them to be ignorant of religion any more than I am raising them to be atheists. I am not telling them that they have to follow my way of thinking, because as a parent, it's my job to encourage them to think for themselves. I know that many religious parents do the same for their kids, and I know that good parenting has no religious affiliation. But how can a parent foster an open and questioning mind in a child who is also told to follow a god—without question?

I am not advocating that religious parents not include their children in the faith they have chosen. But I am urging parents to expose their children to the many other ways, including the way I have chosen: no religion at all. I do not demonize believers to my kids, and I hope that those who follow religion will not present my choice as evil and wrong.

When it comes to religion, it is hard to allow freedom of choice in our offspring because we want them to emulate us. It is unsettling to think that our own kids might believe in things we do not. It is awful to imagine that they would reject that part of who their parents are. But the fear subsides when I hear the wisdom of my daughter, who recently told me, "I don't have to choose what religion I am right now, but I have the choice to choose."

Give Your Kids the Freedom to Make Their Own Choices

Part of being a good parent is allowing our children to become whatever and whoever they become. Watching my children explore the ideas that are out there and grapple with the many, often conflicting, religious views in the world is exciting. They bring new understanding to things—not only for themselves, but for me as well. If my daughter came to me and told me she was joining a church, I would ask her how she reached her decision. But that would be my approach with any of the big decisions in my children's lives. Questioning puts us all on a path to greater understanding.

As my children navigate their teenage years, I know that the understanding will be harder to come by. The questions will get tougher. The answers won't always be what I want to hear.

But I'll keep asking, and I'll encourage my kids to be open and questioning. They might not end up like me, but I'm at peace with the idea that they will end up as themselves.

"What [Richard] Dawkins, [Sam] Harris, and [Daniel] Dennett—along with the other New Atheists—really demand is that society must place itself in the hands of a new and militant atheistic priesthood."

The "New Atheism" Movement Considers Religion Morally Wrong

Albert Mohler

In the following viewpoint, Albert Mohler examines the so-called New Atheism movement, asserting that New Atheists—in particular Richard Dawkins, Sam Harris, and Daniel Dennett— believe that religion is harmful. He maintains that the New Atheists limit the movement's appeal by claiming that religion is evil and by asserting that atheists are more intelligent than those who believe in God. Albert Mohler is the president of the Southern Baptist Theological Seminary.

Albert Mohler, "The New Atheism?" AlbertMohler.com, November 21, 2006. Copyright © 2008, AlbertMohler.com. All rights reserved. Reproduced by permission.

As you read, consider the following questions:

1. According to Albert Mohler, what kind of political and cultural statement does Richard Dawkins make about believing in God?

2. Why does Dawkins feel that kids need to be protected from parents who believe in God, according to the author?

3. Which of the three New Atheists mentioned in Gary Wolf's article in *WIRED* magazine think that belief in God should be substituted with something secular? Why?

2006 has been a big year for atheism. The release of several major books—all widely touted in the media—has put atheism on the front lines of current cultural conversation. Books such as Richard Dawkins' *The God Delusion*, Daniel Dennett's *Breaking the Spell: Religion as a Natural Phenomenon*, and Sam Harris' *Letter to a Christian Nation* are selling by the thousands and prompting hours of conversation on college campuses and in the media.

Now, *WIRED* magazine comes out with a cover story on atheism for its November 2006 issue. In "The New Atheism," *WIRED* contributing editor Gary Wolf explains that this newly assertive form of atheism declares a very simple message: "No heaven. No hell. Just science."

WIRED is itself a cultural symbol for the growing centrality of technology in our lives. On the other hand, the magazine is not simply a celebration of emerging technologies nor a catalogue of soon-to-be-released marvels. Instead, the magazine consistently offers significant intellectual content and it takes on many of the most controversial issues of the times. Considering the relatively young readership of the magazine, the decision to put atheism on the front cover indicates something of where they think the society is headed—at least in interest.

Wolf accomplishes a great deal in his article, thoughtfully introducing the work of militant atheists such as Dawkins, Harris, and Dennett. At the same time, he probes more deeply into the actual meaning of the New Atheism as a movement and a message.

New Atheists Feel That Religion Is Evil

At the beginning of his article, he gets right to the point: "The New Atheists will not let us off the hook simply because we are not doctrinaire believers. They condemn not just belief in God but *respect* for belief in God. Religion is not only wrong; it's evil. Now that the battle has been joined, there's no excuse for shirking."

In order to understand the New Atheism, Wolf traveled to visit with Dawkins, Harris, and Dennett. His interviews with the three are illuminating and analytical.

He met Dawkins in Oxford, which Wolf describes as the "Jerusalem" of human reason. Accordingly, he labels Dawkins "the leading light of the New Atheism movement."

In one sense, this is hardly news. Richard Dawkins, Charles Simonyi Professor of the Public Understanding of Science at Oxford University, has been the most ardent and well-publicized intellectual opponent of Christianity for decades now. He was first famous for the evolutionary argument he presented in his best-selling book, *The Selfish Gene*, now decades old. In his more recent work, Dawkins appears to have left his scientific career something in the background as he attempts to write as something of a philosopher and (a)theologian.

Dawkins' new book, *The God Delusion*, reached the best-seller list in [late 2007], and he has made media appearances on everything from the mainstream media to Comedy Central. Unlike many journalists, Wolf understands what makes Dawkins unique. It is not so much that Dawkins is attempting to convince believers that they should no longer believe in God. To the contrary, Dawkins is attempting a very different cultural and political move. He wants to make *respect for* belief in God socially unacceptable.

"Dawkins is perfectly aware that atheism is an ancient doctrine and that little of what he has to say is likely to change the terms of this stereotyped debate," Wolf writes. "But he continues to go at it. His true interlocutors are not the Christians he confronts directly but the wavering nonbelievers or quasi believers among his listeners—people like me, potential New Atheists who might be inspired by his example."

As Dawkins explains himself, "I'm quite keen on the politics of persuading people of the virtues of atheism." The Oxford professor also understands that atheism is a political issue as well as a theological question. "The number of nonreligious people in the US is something nearer to 30 million than 20 million. That's more than all the Jews in the world put together. I think we're in the same position the gay movement was in a few decades ago. There was a need for people to come out. The more people who came out, the more people who had the courage to come out. I think that's the case with atheists. They're more numerous than anybody realizes."

For a man who is supposedly an exemplar of the humble discipline of science, Dawkins is capable of breathtaking condescension. Consider these words: "Highly intelligent people are mostly atheists. . . . Not a single member of either house of Congress admits to being an atheist. It just doesn't add up. Either they're stupid, or they're lying. And have they got a motive for lying? Of course they've got a motive! Everyone knows that an atheist can't get elected."

Note his argument carefully—highly intelligent people are most likely to be atheists.

Dawkins Argues That Kids Need to Be Protected from Religion

The political dimensions of Dawkins' thought become immediately apparent when he speaks of how children should be protected from parents who believe in God. "How much do we regard children as being the property of their parents?," Dawkins asks. "It's one thing to say people should be free to believe whatever they like, but should they be free to impose their beliefs on their children? Is there something to be said for society to be stepping in? What about bringing up children to believe manifest falsehoods?"

Wolf has successfully captured the essence of what animates Richard Dawkins. He is an evangelist for atheism.

"Evangelism is a moral imperative," Wolf explains. "Dawkins does not merely disagree with religious myths. He disagrees with tolerating them, with cooperating in their colonization of the brains of innocent tykes." As Dawkins sees it, belief in God is a dangerous "meme." Dawkins is famous for arguing that memes serve as a major driving force in evolution. Memes, cultural replicators like ideas, can spread like a virus through society. Wolf understands that Dawkins claims to believe in democracy and freedom and thus accepts "that there are practical constraints on controlling the spread of bad memes." Nevertheless, "Bad ideas foisted on children are moral wrongs. We should think harder about how to stop them."

In a very real sense, Richard Dawkins grabs the headlines precisely because he is willing to say what many other atheists think. Indeed, he is willing to say what other atheists *must* think, but are unwilling to say for one political reason or another. Dawkins is spectacularly unconcerned about public relations.

On the link between evolution and atheism, for example, Dawkins is unrepentant and direct—evolutionary theory *must* logically lead to atheism. While other evolutionists argue be-

Atheism's Message Limits Its Appeal

What accounts for the failure of atheists to organise and wield influence? One problem is that they are hardly a cohesive group. Another issue is simply branding. "Atheist" has an ugly ring in American ears and it merely defines what people are not. "Godless" is worse, its derogatory attachment to "communist" may never be broken. "Humanist" sounds too hippyish.

Economist, "America's Atheists:
Believe It or Not," December 11, 2007.

fore courts and in the media that this is not so, Dawkins states that he cannot worry about the public relations consequences.

No Tolerance for Anything but Complete Atheism

As he told Wolf: "My answer is that the big war is not between evolution and creationism, but between naturalism and supernaturalism. The 'sensible' religious people are really on the side of the fundamentalists, because they believe in supernaturalism. That puts me on the other side." As Wolf explains, Dawkins himself insisted that the word "sensible" should be in quotes. In other words, Dawkins seems to have less respect for theological liberalism than for those who are theologically orthodox. At least the true believers know what they truly believe.

This attack on religious moderates is what made *The End of Faith*, Sam Harris' 2004 book, so interesting. Harris, whose second book, *Letter to a Christian Nation*, was released [in 2007], argues that religious moderates and theological liberals function as something like "enablers" of orthodoxy and fundamentalism. As Wolf keenly observes, the New Atheists oppose agnostics and liberal believers as those who help orthodox believers build and retain a cultural powerbase. Agnostics and theological liberals may be fellow travelers with the atheists, these figures admit, but they actually serve to confuse rather than to clarify the issues at stake. On this, the New Atheists and orthodox believers are in agreement.

Favoring a "Religion of Reason"

Sam Harris is even more apocalyptic than Richard Dawkins or Daniel Dennett. He argues that, unless belief in God is eradicated, civilization is likely to end in a murderous sea of religious warfare. As an alternative, Harris proposes a "religion of reason." As he explains, "We would have realized the rational means to maximize human happiness. We may all agree that we want to have a Sabbath that we take really seriously—a lot more seriously than most religious people take it. But it would be a rational decision, and it would not be just because it's in the Bible. We would be able to invoke the power of poetry and ritual and silent contemplation and all the variables of happiness so that we could exploit them. Call it prayer, but we would have prayer without [expletive deleted]."

Wolf helpfully offers his version of such a prayer: "that our reason will subjugate our superstition, that our intelligence will check our illusions, that we will be able to hold at bay the evil temptation of faith."

Harris' self-proclaimed religion of reason bears uncanny resemblances to the features of New Age thought—something that offends many of his fellow New Atheists. Still, Harris' books have sold by the thousands and he has transformed himself into a poster child for militant atheism. Like Dawkins, Harris sees time on his side. "At some point, there's going to be enough pressure that it is just going to be too *embarrassing* to believe in God."

Belief Is Part of Evolution—and No Longer Necessary

The third major figure in Wolf's article, Daniel Dennett, teaches at Tufts University. As Wolf explains, "Among the New Atheists, Dennett holds an exalted but ambiguous place. Like Dawkins and Harris, he is an evangelizing nonbeliever." Wolf describes Dennett as offering more humorous examples and thought experiments than Dawkins and Harris. "But like the other New Atheists, Dennett gives no quarter to believers who resist subjecting their faith to scientific evaluation. In fact, he argues that neutral, scientifically informed education about every religion in the world should be mandatory in school. After all, he argues, 'if you have to hoodwink—or blindfold—your children to ensure that they confirm their faith when they are adults, your faith *ought* to go extinct.'" Like Harris, Dennett believes that something like a religion of reason might be possible. But, in some contrast to Dawkins and Harris, Dennett does not see faith as something that can be intellectualized away. To the contrary, he sees belief in God to have served an evolutionary purpose. Even as he now believes that evolutionary purpose is no longer helpful, he argues that such an evolutionary feature is not likely to be eradicated quickly. Therefore, Dennett suggests replacing belief in God with something of a secular substitute.

In his wide-ranging article, Wolf considers the emergence of the New Atheism from multiple perspectives. He deals not only with Dawkins, Harris, and Dennett, but with a host of others, including some who believe in God. He understands that the New Atheists stand in contrast with the older atheism more in terms of mood and mode of public engagement. He also understands that those who attempt to rebut the New Atheism on scientific grounds can find themselves facing considerable complexity. As Wolf explains, when defenders of faith accept science as the arbiter of reality, atheists are left "with the upper hand."

Alienating Public with Arrogance

Throughout the article, Wolf also admits his own doubts. He seems to identify himself more with agnosticism than atheism, and he reveals some discomfort with the stridency of the New Atheism.

In his words: "The New Atheists have castigated fundamentalism and branded even the mildest religious liberals as enablers of a vengeful mob. Everybody who does not join them is an ally of the Taliban. But, so far, their provocation has failed to take hold. Given all the religious trauma in the world, I take this as good news. Even those of us who sympathize intellectually have good reasons to wish that the New Atheists continue to seem absurd. If we reject their polemics, if we continue to have respectful conversations even about things we find ridiculous, this doesn't necessarily mean we've lost our convictions or our sanity. It simply reflects our deepest, democratic values. Or, you might say, our bedrock faith: the faith that no matter how confident we are in our beliefs, there's always a chance that we could turn out to be wrong."

The very fact that Wolf remains unconvinced by the arguments promoted by the New Atheists is itself significant. What Dawkins, Harris, and Dennett—along with the other New Atheists—really demand is that society must place itself in the hands of a new and militant atheistic priesthood. Science as defined by these new priests, would serve as the new sacrament and as the means of salvation.

What this article reveals is that those arguing that human beings need to be saved *from* belief in God are facing a tough sell—even in *WIRED* magazine.

Periodical Bibliography

The following articles have been selected to supplement the diverse views presented in this chapter.

Gary Bauer	"Why Religion (Still) Matters," May 18, 2007. www.humanevents.com.
Andrew Brown	"Why God Can't Not Exist," *New Statesman*, November 13, 2006.
William Lane Craig	"God Is Not Dead Yet: How Current Philosophers Argue for His Existence," *Christianity Today*, July 2008.
Dina Davis	"Olivia's Story: Helping a Young Freethinker Blossom," *Freethought Today*, April 2008.
Richard Dawkins	"Religion's Real Child Abuse," May 15, 2006. www.richarddawkins.net.
Rich Deem	"Is the Teaching of Religion Really a Form of Child Abuse?" December 28, 2007. www.godandscience.org.
Moses Mapesa	"Why Religious Education Cannot Be Compulsory," *Africa News Service*, July 23, 2008.
Jon Meacham	"Is God Real?" *Newsweek*, April 9, 2007.
Bradford R. Pilcher	"Dear God, You're Fired," *American Jewish Life Magazine*, March-April 2007.
Stephen Prothero	"American Faith: A Work in Progress," *USA Today*, March 10, 2008.

CHAPTER 2

What Is Atheism's Impact on Society?

Chapter Preface

There has been—and continues to be—much debate over the impact of atheism on society. Nowhere has this been more apparent than in the arguments over whether the religious aspects of Christmas have been lost as a result of secularism in general and atheism in particular. These arguments about Christmas mirror much of the same animosity that has marked the larger battle over what role—if any—religion should play in society.

Some religious Christians feel that there has been a concerted effort on the part of atheists and secularists to dilute the true nature of Christmas. The phrase "Keep Christ in Christmas" has been repeated often in recent years, as religious Christians fight back against what they maintain is an effort to rid the United States of any vestige of religion.

John Gibson's 2005 book *The War on Christmas: How the Liberal Plot to Ban the Sacred Christian Holiday Is Worse than You Thought* describes the fear of many Christians that the religious nature of Christmas is being suppressed and threatened.

Among several examples, Gibson cites the effort of the American Civil Liberties Union (ACLU) to prevent the word "Christmas" from being used to describe the two-week vacation period in December in the Covington, Georgia, school district. "In aggressively trying to stamp out any semblance of Christianity in a place it finds Christianity abhorrent (in the presence of schoolchildren), the ACLU was asking people to ignore the obvious, to pretend they did not know why the school break was taking place."

Those who believe that religion should not play a role in everyday society contend that there is not a plot to dilute Christmas; they assert, rather, that there should be an acknowledgement that not everyone celebrates Christmas. In an article for the *Washington Post*, Ruth Marcus writes, "There is an ugly, bullying aspect to this dispute, in which the pro-Christmas forces are not only asking, reasonably, that their religion be treated with equal status and respect but in which they are attacking legitimate efforts at inclusivity. It's this sense of aggrieved victimhood that confuses me: What, exactly, is so threatening about calling the school holiday a winter break rather than Christmas vacation?"

The disputes over the extent to which the religious aspects of Christmas should be celebrated in public include calling a Christmas tree a "holiday tree," greeting people with "Happy Holidays" instead of "Merry Christmas," displaying crèches on public property, and singing Christmas songs in public schools.

Those who support public expressions of religion contend that taking the religion out of Christmas will weaken the United States morally. On the Human Events Web site, Don Feder writes, "Christianity is all that stands in the way of the left's cherished goals—to make America like Europe (whose leaders can't even acknowledge the continent's Christian heritage in the proposed constitution for the European Union), like Sweden (that almost imprisoned a pastor for preaching the Biblical view of homosexuality), like the Netherlands (that has legalized euthanasia, prostitution, group marriage and drugs), like France (whose natives have negative population growth which, when combined with open-borders and generous welfare benefits, is creating an Islamic republic of the future), like—San Francisco, Times Square and Berkeley all rolled into one."

Opponents of open displays of religion in public counter by stating that the morality of the United States is better gauged by other actions. Writing on *The Huffington Post*, Eric Williams argues, "Americans are not losing their homes or paying fifty bucks to fill up the tank because there's no manger in the town square or Ten Commandments on the courthouse wall. Our morality is demonstrated by our actions in Guantanamo and New Orleans, not by whether the clerk at Costco says 'Happy Holidays' rather than 'Merry Christmas.'"

The divide between those who contend that religion is threatened by atheism and those who maintain that religion endangers the secular nature of society is debated by the authors in the following chapter about the impact of atheism on society.

> *"An honest person wants solid evidence to support assertions, and is leery of baseless claims. Therefore, skeptics are the most honest of all."*

Atheism Benefits Society

James A. Haught

In the following viewpoint, James A. Haught argues that it is dishonest to believe that religion can explain everything in life. He maintains that secularism and atheism benefit society because they use evidence to prove their beliefs, while religion claims to provide answers in traditions and beliefs for which there is no evidence. Haught, the editor in chief of the Charleston Gazette *in West Virginia, wrote this article for* Freethought Today, *which is published by the Freedom from Religion Foundation, an organization devoted to the separation of church and state.*

As you read, consider the following questions:

1. According to James Haught, how did his high school chemistry class show him that science can explain everything that religion cannot?

James A. Haught, "It's All About Honesty," *Freethought Today*, vol. 24, November 2007. © 2007 Freedom From Religion Foundation. Reproduced by permission.

2. How does "the Problem of Evil" challenge common religious beliefs, according to the author?

3. In Haught's opinion, why are skeptics more honest than people who do not seek evidence and reason?

Nobody actually knows where beliefs come from. Psychologists can't explain what makes some people religious skeptics and others believers—or why some become conformists and others become rebels, or political conservatives and liberals, or war "hawks" and peace "doves," or puritans and playboys, or death penalty advocates and opponents, etc.

Therefore, I don't know what caused me to be a doubter while my classmates were believers, some even becoming preachers. All I know is my own story:

I was born in 1932 in a little West Virginia farm town that had no electricity or paved streets. My family had gaslights, but farmers outside town lived with kerosene lamps, woodstoves, and outdoor toilets.

Science Offers More Answers than Religion

I was sent to Bible Belt Sunday Schools, and tried to pray as a child. But an awakening occurred in my teen years. In high school chemistry class, I learned how gaps and surpluses in outer electron shells cause atoms to bind into molecules, making almost everything in our world. It was a revelation explaining much of existence. Science became an obsession, a portal to understanding reality. Slowly, religion's claims of invisible gods, devils, heavens, hells, angels, demons, miracles and messiahs turned into fairy tales.

Rather by accident, I lucked into a newspaper job, and my world expanded. A cynical city editor laughed at "holy rollers" and huckster evangelists. We debated religion. I agreed that supernatural church claims are baloney—but I had a quandary: If the magical explanations are nonsense, I asked, what

The Search for Honesty in Religion

Every one of the world's "great" religions utterly trivializes the immensity and beauty of the cosmos. Books like the Bible and the Koran get almost every significant fact about us and our world wrong. Every scientific domain—from cosmology to psychology to economics—has superseded and surpassed the wisdom of Scripture.

Everything of value that people get from religion can be had more honestly, without presuming anything on insufficient evidence. The rest is self-deception, set to music.

Sam Harris, "God's Dupes,"
Los Angeles Times, *March 15, 2007.*

better answers exist? Why is the universe here? Why do we live and die? Is there any purpose to it all? Is everything random? What can an honest person say? What answer can a person of integrity give?

He eyed me sharply and replied: "You can say: I don't know." Bingo! Immediately, a path of honesty opened for me. Previously, I had sensed that it's dishonest for theologians to claim supernatural knowledge without any proof, but I had lacked a truthful alternative. Now I had one. I could quit agonizing and admit that ultimate mysteries are unknowable.

History Tells Us Why We Should Be Skeptical

I joined a skeptical Unitarian group, read physics and philosophy books, and cemented a scientific worldview. Beliefs should rest on intelligent evidence, not on fables. Eventually, I saw seven logical reasons why thinking people should reject church dogmas:

- Horrible occurrences such as the Indian Ocean tsunami that drowned 100,000 children prove clearly that the universe isn't administered by an all-loving invisible father. No compassionate creator would devise killer earthquakes and hurricanes—or breast cancer for women and leukemia for children—or hawks to rip rabbits apart and pythons to crush pigs and sharks to slaughter seals. A creator who concocted such things would be crueler than people are. In philosophy, this dilemma is called the Problem of Evil. It doesn't disprove the existence of a heartless god, but it wipes out the merciful god of churches.

- Hundreds of past gods and religions have vanished, and are laughable today. Zeus' Pantheon atop Mount Olympus was so real to ancient Greeks that they sacrificed thousands of animals to the imaginary gods and goddesses. Are today's deities any more substantial?

- Although churches claim that religion makes believers loving and brotherly, the historic record shows opposite results. Human sacrifice, holy wars, Inquisition torture chambers, massacres of heretics, Crusades against infidels, witch hunts, Reformation wars, pogroms against Jews, Jonestown, Waco, nerve gas in Tokyo's subway, suicide bombings by today's Muslim fanatics—all these undercut the kindly image of believers.

- Most of the brightest thinkers throughout history— philosophers, scientists, writers, democracy reformers, and other "greats"—have been skeptics. Omar Khayyam, Michel de Montaigne, William Shakespeare, Voltaire, Thomas Jefferson, Benjamin Franklin, Thomas

Paine, Ralph Waldo Emerson, Henry David Thoreau, Charles Darwin, Leo Tolstoy, Mark Twain, Thomas Edison, Luther Burbank, Sigmund Freud, Bertrand Russell, Albert Einstein, Margaret Sanger, Will Durant, Jean-Paul Sartre, Isaac Asimov, Kurt Vonnegut, Carl Sagan—this is illustrious company. If the best minds couldn't swallow supernatural tenets, why should we?

- Scientific thinking requires detectable, testable evidence. But religion offers no proof except writings left by long-dead holy men. Muhammad said the angel Gabriel dictated the Koran to him. That's proof enough for a billion Muslims. Joseph Smith, a convicted fraud artist, said an angel named Moroni helped him find buried golden tablets, which he translated into miracle-filled scriptures. That's proof enough for millions of Mormons. But honest seekers need something more tangible.

- Despite the common assumption that church leaders are more moral than ordinary folks, a horrifying number of ministers and priests are child-molesters, swindlers, adulterers, or half-cracked charlatans. A few even commit murder. There's no evidence that religion makes them holier than thou.

- All church predictions of miraculous events have been flops. Millerites waited on hilltops for a Second Coming that didn't come. Jehovah's Witnesses set several wrong dates for Doomsday. Fundamentalists thought the 2000 millennium passage would bring heavenly havoc. The Rapture probably will be another rupture.

Over the years, I've spelled out these premises in seven books and 60 magazine essays. I even hatched a freethought novel focused on religious absurdities in ancient Greece.

Honesty and Evidence Are Needed

To me, the bottom line is honesty. A person with integrity doesn't claim to know supernatural things that he or she doesn't know. An honest person wants solid evidence to support assertions, and is leery of baseless claims. Therefore, skeptics are the most honest of all.

> *"The indisputable fact is that all the religions of the world put together have in 2,000 years not managed to kill as many people as have been killed in the name of atheism in the past few decades."*

Atheism Harms Society

Dinesh D'Souza

In the following viewpoint, Dinesh D'Souza argues that religion has been unfairly blamed for being responsible for the deaths of many, while dictators such as Adolf Hitler and Joseph Stalin murdered millions of people in their attempts to establish a world without religion. While D'Souza acknowledges that violence has been used in the name of religion, he contends that religion—unlike atheism—offers a set of morals that denounce the killing of innocent people. D'Souza's books include What's So Great About Christianity, Letters to a Young Conservative, *and* The Enemy at Home: The Cultural Left and Its Responsibility for 9/11.

Dinesh D'Souza, "Atheism, Not Religion, Is the Real Force Behind the Mass Murders of History," *Christian Science Monitor*, November 21, 2006. Reproduced by permission of the author.

As you read, consider the following questions:

1. In Dinesh D'Souza's opinion, how did Adolf Hitler, Joseph Stalin, and Mao Zedong justify the number of people killed during their regimes?
2. According to the author, what motivates many so-called religious battles, such as that between Israel and the Palestinians?
3. Who does atheism view as "the creator of values," in D'Souza's opinion?

A spate of atheist books have argued that religion represents, as *The End of Faith* author Sam Harris puts it, "the most potent source of human conflict, past and present."

Columnist Robert Kuttner gives the familiar litany. "The Crusades slaughtered millions in the name of Jesus. The Inquisition brought the torture and murder of millions more. After Martin Luther, Christians did bloody battle with other Christians for another three centuries."

In his bestseller *The God Delusion*, Richard Dawkins contends that most of the world's recent conflicts—in the Middle East, in the Balkans, in Northern Ireland, in Kashmir, and in Sri Lanka—show the vitality of religion's murderous impulse.

More People Have Been Murdered in the Name of Atheism

The problem with this critique is that it exaggerates the crimes attributed to religion, while ignoring the greater crimes of secular fanaticism. The best example of religious persecution in America is the Salem witch trials. How many people were killed in those trials? Thousands? Hundreds? Actually, fewer than 25. Yet the event still haunts the liberal imagination.

It is strange to witness the passion with which some secular figures rail against the misdeeds of the Crusaders and Inquisitors more than 500 years ago. The number sentenced to death by the Spanish Inquisition appears to be about 10,000. Some historians contend that an additional 100,000 died in jail due to malnutrition or illness.

These figures are tragic, and of course population levels were much lower at the time. But even so, they are minuscule compared with the death tolls produced by the atheist despotisms of the 20th century. In the name of creating their version of a religion-free utopia, Adolf Hitler, Joseph Stalin, and Mao Zedong produced the kind of mass slaughter that no Inquisitor could possibly match. Collectively these atheist tyrants murdered more than 100 million people.

Moreover, many of the conflicts that are counted as "religious wars" were not fought over religion. They were mainly fought over rival claims to territory and power. Can the wars between England and France be called religious wars because the English were Protestants and the French were Catholics? Hardly.

The same is true today. The Israeli-Palestinian conflict is not, at its core, a religious one. It arises out of a dispute over self-determination and land. Hamas and the extreme orthodox parties in Israel may advance theological claims—"God gave us this land" and so forth—but the conflict would remain essentially the same even without these religious motives. Ethnic rivalry, not religion, is the source of the tension in Northern Ireland and the Balkans.

Religion Teaches Morality

Yet today's atheists insist on making religion the culprit. Consider Mr. Harris's analysis of the conflict in Sri Lanka. "While the motivations of the Tamil Tigers are not explicitly religious," he informs us, "they are Hindus who undoubtedly believe many improbable things about the nature of life and death." In other words, while the Tigers see themselves as combatants in a secular political struggle, Harris detects a reli-

Religion Tells Us That Man Is Not God

It is not religion that makes men fanatics; it is the power of the human desire for justice, so often partisan and perverted. That fanatical desire can be found in both religion and atheism. In the contest between religion and atheism, the strength of religion is to recognize two apparently contrary forces in the human soul: the power of injustice and the power, nonetheless, of our desire for justice. The stubborn existence of injustice reminds us that man is not God, while the demand for justice reminds us that we wish for the divine. Religion tries to join these two forces together.

Harvey Mansfield, "Atheist Tracts,"
The Weekly Standard, *August 13, 2007, p. 13.*

gious motive because these people happen to be Hindu and surely there must be some underlying religious craziness that explains their fanaticism.

Harris can go on forever in this vein. Seeking to exonerate secularism and atheism from the horrors perpetrated in their name, he argues that Stalinism and Maoism were in reality "little more than a political religion." As for Nazism, "while the hatred of Jews in Germany expressed itself in a predominantly secular way, it was a direct inheritance from medieval Christianity." Indeed, "The holocaust marked the culmination of . . . two thousand years of Christian fulminating against the Jews."

One finds the same inanities in Mr. Dawkins's work. Don't be fooled by this rhetorical legerdemain [sleight of hand]. Dawkins and Harris cannot explain why, if Nazism was directly descended from medieval Christianity, medieval Christianity did not produce a Hitler. How can a self-proclaimed atheist ideology, advanced by Hitler as a repudiation of Christianity, be a "culmination" of 2,000 years of Christianity? Dawkins and Harris are employing a transparent sleight of hand that holds Christianity responsible for the crimes committed in its name, while exonerating secularism and atheism for the greater crimes committed in their name.

Religion Offers a Moral Code

Religious fanatics have done things that are impossible to defend, and some of them, mostly in the Muslim world, are still performing horrors in the name of their creed. But if religion sometimes disposes people to self-righteousness and absolutism, it also provides a moral code that condemns the slaughter of innocents. In particular, the moral teachings of Jesus provide no support for—indeed they stand as a stern rebuke to—the historical injustices perpetrated in the name of Christianity.

The crimes of atheism have generally been perpetrated through a hubristic ideology that sees man, not God, as the creator of values. Using the latest techniques of science and technology, man seeks to displace God and create a secular utopia here on earth. Of course if some people—the Jews, the landowners, the unfit, or the handicapped—have to be eliminated in order to achieve this utopia, this is a price the atheist tyrants and their apologists have shown themselves quite willing to pay. Thus they confirm the truth of Fyodor Dostoyevsky's dictum, "If God is not, everything is permitted."

Whatever the motives for atheist bloodthirstiness, the indisputable fact is that all the religions of the world put together have in 2,000 years not managed to kill as many people as have been killed in the name of atheism in the past few decades.

It's time to abandon the mindlessly repeated mantra that religious belief has been the greatest source of human conflict and violence. Atheism, not religion, is the real force behind the mass murders of history.

> *"[Atheists'] paradise is an earth on which no supernatural claims control the lives of men and women, a planet on which reality rules in the decisions that shape the course of human events."*

Society Does Not Need Religion

Frank R. Zindler

In the following viewpoint, Frank R. Zindler argues that improving public education can help lead to a society that doesn't need to depend on religious beliefs and traditions. He also maintains that the information disseminated by the Internet, as well as the broadcast and print media, must be improved to balance the incorrect information about atheism that is spread by the government and places of worship. Frank R. Zindler is the acting president of American Atheists, which was founded by Madalyn Murray O'Hair and is devoted to protecting the civil rights of atheists.

As you read, consider the following questions:

1. According to Frank Zindler, why do some people believe that religiosity is a part of human DNA?

Frank R. Zindler, "A World Without Religion—How Will It Be Achieved?" *American Atheist Magazine*, vol. 43, Summer 2005, p. 4. Copyright © 2005 American Atheists inc. Reproduced by permission.

2. Why did Thomas Jefferson contend that public education is vital to keeping church and state separate, according to the author?

3. In Zindler's opinion, what caused atheism to become associated with communism?

No Atheist believes in hell or eternal punishment. No Atheist believes in gods or goddesses or supernatural beings of any kind—malevolent or benevolent. No Atheist believes in spirits, souls, or reincarnation. Nevertheless, many Atheists fervently believe in heaven—perhaps paradise would be a more accurate term.

Unlike the paradise of the Muslims and Christians, the paradise they envision is a physical world, a realm in which "religion" is no more than a curious word in their dictionaries. Their paradise is an earth on which no supernatural claims control the lives of men and women, a planet on which reality rules in the decisions that shape the course of human events.

Atheists' Heaven Does Not Depend on Religious Faith

The heaven for which Atheists hope is a land in which the quarreling divisions created by racist religions have been replaced by a humanity united in its resolve to labor together to achieve a global society in which all are treated fairly and all fairly share in the bounty of the soil from which our species sprang so long ago.

The heaven for which Atheists strive is not a world in which there are no problems to solve, nor even a world in which no disasters or tragedies occur. Rather, it is a world in which finding solutions to life's problems is not impeded by benighted and obstructionist taboos and superstitions or blocked by the willful ignorance that everywhere is the hallmark and ensign of religious faith. It is a world in which tragedies and disasters are not of human design but are simply the consequence of living in a universe that was not made for us—an unconscious cosmos, which decrees no destinies nor plans any products, but evolves inexorably under quantum-mechanical conditions whereby even the most implausible event may eventually occur.

There may be pain in the Atheists' paradise, but it is pain of the unavoidable sort. The pain of Holy Roman Inquisitions, the pain of Jews, Christians, and Hindus killing Muslims who are killing Christians, Jews, and Hindus, the agony of Christian Scientists killing their children with prayer overdose, the religious wars and persecutions that make the misery of so many lives—these all are absent in the religion-free Elysium [a place of perfect happiness] of which we Atheists dream.

That is the Valhalla [a heaven-like destiny] to which Atheist heroes and heroines aspire. That is the paradise they plan for their progeny—the heavenly heritage they hope to bequeath to a rational race of the future.

Do Atheists wish in vain? Is a world without religion possible? If it is possible, how is it to be achieved? And finally, would it resemble the paradise described above?

It has been argued that religiosity is part of humanity's sociobiological inheritance, that natural selection has favored genes for religiosity as part of a behavioral genetic package that gave the greatest advantage to tribal societies in which religion was a cohesive force enabling them better to exterminate the genetic competition. The fact that almost 40% of American scientists still adhere to religious beliefs of some kind lends credibility to the notion that there is a genetic bias which can override the rational faculties of even well-educated and otherwise rational people. It is doubtful, however, that 40% of humanity is irredeemably religious. In Western Europe, the former Soviet Union, China, and Japan the percentage of persons mentally scarred by religious modes of thought is much, much smaller. It would appear that a world essentially free of delusion is possible.

What would that world be like? Would a world devoid of transcendental temptations resemble Eden without the snake? It all depends on how a religion-free world is attained.

Education Is the Key to Independent Thinking

If the world as a whole could evolve on the Western European model, where education has been effective in instilling naturalistic modes of thinking and thinking becomes almost reflexively skeptical and critical, paradise will be achieved with minimal difficulty. Scandinavia seems almost there already. Some legal changes only need to be made to disestablish the moribund churches so that they can shrivel away to complete oblivion. In this scenario, there need be no violence, no repression of atavistic individuals who still traffic in supernatural claims and wares. Increasingly, priests and preachers will find fewer customers willing to pay their rent in advance to reserve condominiums in heaven.

In trying to predict the future it is helpful to look for lessons in the past. It may be instructive to compare the different ways in which America and the Soviet Union traveled the road to reason—if possible to see why both have failed ultimately, even though both progressed along that road a great distance early in their histories.

In the case of America, the American Revolution took place at the height of the Enlightenment, when science and reason were shining their light upon religion and causing it to wither like a cave fungus exposed to the fervent lumination of the sun. Even more important, religion was fragmented at the time and did not create a major impediment to revolution. Only one of the many churches present in the colonies was closely associated with the British Crown, against which the American revolutionaries had to wage war. The Founding Fa-

Religion Is a Threat to Our Integrity

The better is enemy of the best: religion may make many people better, but it is preventing them from being as good as they could be. If only we could transfer all that respect, loyalty and intense devotion from an imaginary being—God—to something real: the wonderful world of goodness we and our ancestors have made, and of which we are now the stewards.

Daniel Dennett and Robert Winston,
"Is Religion a Threat to Rationality and Science?"
The Guardian, *April 22, 2008.*

thers of the American republic did not have to wage war against priests and preachers as well as the king in order to gain their freedom. After the success of the revolution, when an unprecedented, intentionally and utterly godless constitution was proposed, the warring sects could understand that it was in their own best interest not to have an established religion.

The enlightened composers of the secular charter probably believed privately that religion would gradually decline and be replaced by a humanistic, rational philosophy. Thomas Jefferson, however, realized that this was far from inevitable, and he saw the crucial role of public education in maintaining a godless government wherein church and state remained separate:

"Every government degenerates when trusted to the rulers of the people alone. The people themselves are its only safe depositories. And to render even them safe, their minds must be improved to a certain degree. . . . An amendment of our constitution must here come in aid of the public education."

Atheism Was Unfairly Linked to Communism

Up until the second half of the nineteenth century, until the time of the Civil War, education seems to have been largely effective, and free thought and even outright Atheism flourished as never since. Crowds of people actually paid large amounts of money to hear "The Great Agnostic" Robert Ingersoll lecture, and he died a wealthy man in 1899. In fact, education in America seems to have continued to prepare improved minds up until World War II. It was only with the development of the Cold War that American public education fell prey to religion as the nation struggled against "Godless Communism." Suddenly, Americanism was identified with religiosity and Atheism was identified with Communism—and Communism was un-American. Since then, American education has continued to decline, and the United States has now sunken to the level of religious sophistication of the Age of Inquisitions.

In the case of the Russian Revolution, things were quite different. In Russia, religion was monolithic and inseparable from the Czarist government against which the revolutionaries had to struggle. It was not possible to fight the Czar without also fighting against the Russian Orthodox Patriarch. As a practical necessity, religion had to be suppressed if the world envisioned by the revolutionists were to become a reality. Alas, compulsory education in Atheism was never able to eradicate the roots of superstition from the Soviet people, even though the ruling class was largely free of religious ideation. As the government became ever more repressive in its attempts to stay in power, even though religion was only one of many things being suppressed, it became the rallying point of the resistance and attracted all who had legitimate objections to the ruling regime. When at last the Soviet system imploded, religion was a major component of the gases and vapors which rushed in to fill the void created by the disappearance of the secular government. Today, creationists, astrologers, faith-healers, Mormons, Jehovah's Witnesses, and charlatans of every stripe are picnicking everywhere from the Baltic to the Steppes of Central Asia, and Muslim fundamentalists are leading what from afar seems to be a second Russian revolution.

Will the Atheists' heaven be attained by the American, Soviet, or West-European method, or will some other means be required? We have already noted that the American and Soviet routes to reason have failed, even though in their earlier stages they achieved considerable success. It is disturbing to note that the West-European model also is now exhibiting considerable signs of strain.

Pacifying the Religious Will Only Lead to Fanaticism

The presence of multitudes of Muslims in France—the land of Voltaire, d'Holbach, and Dupuis—has made it necessary to prohibit religious garb and symbols in the public schools. This has been widely denounced even by freethinkers who do not seem to realize that failure to defend secularism—by tolerating the intolerant and by embracing those who seek the destruction of secular government—is tantamount to societal suicide. Can a society be so free that it allows its citizens to abolish freedom?

In the Netherlands, where even the Roman Catholic Church and the Calvinists have been tamed and are no more sanguinary than sedated hamsters, a Muslim fundamentalist recently assassinated a Dutch filmmaker who dared to criticize Muslim misogyny. (We all remember too the Salman Rushdie affair, where even today the 1989 fatwah of the Ayatollah Khomeini has not been disavowed by the Muslim communities of America and Europe.) There are now nearly a million Muslims in that tiny nation. How can Dutch secular society survive? It appears that education is failing in Holland and that, as in America, parochial education is churning out fanatical, politically radicalized religious know-nothings.

In every part of the world in which even the slightest promise of an Atheistic Utopia has flickered in the consciousness of thinking men and women, hopes are being dashed by the recrudescence of religious fundamentalisms. The violent nature of these fundamentalisms—whether they be Christian, Muslim, Hindu, or even Jewish—bodes ill for those who hope to build bridges to heaven using American or West-European blueprints. Increasingly, there grows the fear that the road to reason will have to be built upon the Soviet model if violent fundamentalisms are to be subdued and even a semblance of democracy is to be preserved.

I suggest that the path that will be followed depends upon the failure or success of education—not just the education occurring in schools and colleges, but also the education gained from the print and broadcast media, the Internet, and the daily interactions of Atheists and Humanists with the larger society. The schools are failing not so much because they are teaching things that are untrue—although there is certainly a lot of nonsense that can be found in what is taught in many places—but that the truth about the world is being drowned in a flood of disinformation gushing out of churches, mosques, temples, moneyed interests, and governments. Those who would broadcast truth to the uninformed and the misinformed are faced with a horrific signal-to-noise ratio problem. The signals of science and reason are swamped by the noise of religion, superstition, willful ignorance, and the credos of credulity.

Reason and Science Must Be Supported by the Government

Without any evidence in its support, many Atheists confidently believe that truth will ultimately prevail. Even so great a thinker as Thomas Jefferson wrote in his *Notes on Virginia* that "Reason and experiment have been indulged, and error has fled before them. It is error alone which needs the support of government. Truth can stand by itself."

It is painful to argue that one of my greatest heroes could have been wrong on so basic an issue, but I must respectfully disagree. Truth, too, needs the support of government if it is not to be choked in a new Noah's Flood of falsehoods. Truth needs also the support of Atheists, Humanists, Rationalists, and Freethinkers of all kinds, but it needs even more if it is to prevail and a new day of enlightenment is to dawn. We all must help truth keep afloat in the flood of fantasy that gushes forth on all sides. It is up to us to solve the signal-to-noise problem so reality awareness can be propagated amongst the masses. We must make our governments realize that it is in their own ultimate interest to side with science against superstition, knowledge against ignorance, reality against illusion, and reason against raw emotion.

The future of the world now depends upon us. Whether we shall progress to the paradise proposed at the beginning of this editorial or descend into a hellish Hades such as Khomeini's Iran, Calvin's Geneva, Torquemada's Toledo, or Cotton Mather's Salem—or worse—depends upon our ability to find a solution to the signal-to-noise problem. No greater problem confronts our reasoning race. No greater emergency calls for our aid. No urgency has ever been more urgent.

"Seldom do they [atheists] rise to a painstaking examination of a serious problem, one that in history or ethics or religion has for centuries driven philosophical struggles into the unknown."

Society Needs Religion

Michael J. Buckley

In the following viewpoint, Michael J. Buckley argues that the inability of atheists to prove that God does not exist is evidence that society needs religion to lead questioning and informed individuals. He contends that atheists make the claim that God does not exist as though it is fact and then find or build the evidence they need to make this accusation. Buckley is a professor of theology at Santa Clara University in Santa Clara, California.

As you read, consider the following questions:

1. In Michael Buckley's opinion, why is it wrong for atheists to state that "God does not exist" without first collecting evidence to support this statement?

2. What are the names of three nineteenth century atheists?

Michael J. Buckley, "The Madman and the Crowd: For the New Atheists, God Is Not Worth a Decent Argument," *America*, vol. 198, May 5, 2008, p. 27. Copyright © 2008 www.americamagazine.org. All rights reserved. Reproduced by permission of America Press. For subscription information, visit www.americamagazine.org.

3. According to the author, how does the "new atheism" differ from the "old atheism"?

Gertrude Stein lay dying. Stomach cancer had finally forced her to undergo surgery in an American hospital on the fringes of Paris. Preparing for the operation, she asked her lifelong companion, Alice B. Toklas, "What is the answer?"

Alice said nothing. Time passed. Gertrude spoke again: "In that case, what is the question?" Attendants came to move her cot into the operating room. Alice never saw her again.

Professor Herbert Lamm loved to repeat the story. He thought her last words a triumph: "That's the smartest thing that woman ever said."

Over the centuries, questions have shaped the development of human beings and their culture. Latent or confused, they have opened up new lines of inquiry and spurred progress. Most human enterprises recognize themselves to be as vital as their questions.

A Superficial Look at a Serious Question

The absence of probing questions may well warrant a sweeping indictment of the "new atheism." It is an astonishing world, one with clever moments but with none of the searching, troubled inquiry in which human beings must "wrestle with the concept," as [German philosopher Georg Wilhelm Friedrich] Hegel put it. Christopher Hitchens once promised that his questions would be resolved by evidence in contrast to religious faith, but there seems little attempt to secure adequate evidence or to present it cogently. Much of his argument amounts to zingers. His new atheist peers use similar strategies. "We know," writes Sam Harris, "that no [italics in original] evidence would be sufficient to authenticate many of the pope's core beliefs. How could anyone born in the twentieth century come to know that Jesus was actually born of a virgin?" So much for the facile weighing of religious literary forms and the happy hegemony of evidence. A literalist reading of the Christian story of creation, or of the ages of the earth, or of the genealogies of the infancy narratives or of the reconstruction of the passion and resurrection of Christ easily sets the stage for ridicule through shallow and clumsy commentary.

Many of these attempts confront the question with the answers already in hand. Seldom do they rise to a painstaking examination of a serious problem, one that in history or ethics or religion has for centuries driven philosophical struggles into the unknown. Little discussion can emerge out of Sam Harris's judgment (which Christopher Hitchens reports with approval): "While religious people are not generally mad, their core beliefs absolutely are." The question is lost. Unfortunately, comprehensive invective does not supply a serious substitute.

Even here, however, the religious intellect may still find significant engagement. Until this current spate of books made its appearance in popular culture, was the reality of God taken as an admissible question in popular circles? As noted by the *Wall Street Journal*, the new champions of atheism have sold close to a million books. The question of God has seldom been argued more publicly than in these latter decades. It is being raised in the strength of its denial. Do honest convictions deepen if they are forced to pursue one of the problems with which St. Thomas opens the *Summa Theologiae*, "Whether God exists"?

What must figure in this matter is the commitment to the absolute in an intellectual honesty that is itself an unqualified subservience to truth. If these claims of the non-negotiable in human experience are not in some oblique way an experience of God, then do human beings have some experiences that are more demanding than the experience of God? Does the question of God itself in its absolute quality bear the evidence for its own resolution?

Answering the Question Before It Has Been Asked

Closely allied to the new atheists' weakness in questioning is a cognate failure in arguments and method. Atheism has historically favored the contradictions of debate. As in Roman rhetoric, so it is today. The spate of books carrying the water for the new atheism begins not with a question to be explored but with the conclusions to be sustained. One begins with the answer: that God does not exist. The task of the author is to collect or construct evidence to support this thesis. Anything can be made to serve, so the contemporary arguments inevitably wander across the pages and often lack simple coherence. Hitchens's argument from metaphysics runs the gamut from naming scientists who happened to be religious to medieval arguments about the length of angels' wings to quarrels between the papacy and the emperor, finishing with a grand finale on the notion of a leap of faith. All of this is placed within a single chapter on "the metaphysical claims of 'religion.'"

Serious inquiry, by contrast, moves in the opposite direction: it begins with the question and then looks for the evidence or arguments that can resolve it. Concern about question and method in the discussion of the existence of God is not a pedantic nicety. It is required if one is to think carefully through the great issues raised by contemporary atheism, and it urges the directive primacy of the question and its care. The central challenge is not that someone has denied the existence of God. In one form or another that denial has been with us for millennia. The central challenge is that much of the eristic manner of interchange has so corrupted the question and the method as to make discussion impossible.

[Richard] Dawkins transmutes the question of God into the question of religion, but seems to think the question of religion comprises not the beginning of universities and hospitals, nor the cathedral of Florence and the music of Pal-

God Must Exist

What would a world without God look like? Well, for one, morality becomes, if not impossible, exceedingly difficult. "Thou shalt not kill" loses much of its force when reduced from commandment to a suggestion. How inspiring can it be to wake in the morning, look in the mirror, and see an accident of evolutionary history—the end product of the random collision of molecules?

Don Feder, "Atheism Isn't the Final Word,"
USA Today, *April 16, 2007.*

estrina, nor a pervasive care for the poor and the suffering, but instead an index of evil events and stupid choices throughout history. His selection of "examples," however overstated, instantiates what the history of rhetoric has asserted over thousands of years: that the choice and marshaling of examples is the induction of the sophist. A thesis can be asserted, or a list constructed and examples selected to prove anything.

Contempt for God and Religious Beliefs

The inadequacies of the new atheism lie not only in its failure to keep the integrity and depth of its question or to sustain an effective methodology with which the question of God could be credibly pursued. There is also an astonishing theological illiteracy that runs through all of these works, an illiteracy that invites comparison with the great atheistic thinkers of the 19th century, such as Ludwig Feuerbach, Arthur Schopenhauer or George Eliot. One representative will have to suffice. The most serious and paradigmatic of the great atheisms of the past century was that of Friedrich Nietzsche; probably his most celebrated advancement of the atheistic option was his parable of the madman in the marketplace, which I relay here with comment.

> Have you not heard of that madman who lit a lantern in the bright morning hours, ran to the marketplace, and cried incessantly: "I seek God! I seek God!" The people in the marketplace convulsed with laughter and screamed mocking questions after the madman: "Has he got lost?" asked one. "Did he lose his way like a child?" asks another. "Or is he hiding?"
>
> Only the madman can answer this question: "I will tell you. We have killed Him—you and I. All of us are his murderers." The full enormity of the deed and of their loss breaks in upon them. "But how did we do this? How could we drink up the sea? Who gave us the sponge to wipe away the entire horizon? What were we doing when we unchained this earth from its sun? Whither is it moving now? Whither are we moving? Away from all suns.... God is dead. God remains dead. And we have killed Him. How shall we comfort ourselves, the murderers of all murderers? What was holiest and mightiest of all the world has yet owned has bled to death under our knives.... Is not the greatness of this deed too great for us?"

The people in the marketplace did not believe that God exists; they thought the search absurd. But for Nietzsche, the determining factor was that they had no understanding of what they had done and what they had lost. They took their disbelief for granted, held faith in contempt, and had no sensible awareness of the new emptiness. The death of God existed among them, but it was an epistemological reality, not an ontological one; Hitchens misses this point completely. The death of God in Nietzsche means that Christian belief was no longer believable. Only the madman knew the unspeakable value of what had been destroyed.

77

It is here in the marketplace that the new atheism both resembles and differs from the old. The new atheists possess contempt for religious belief, but theirs is the contempt of the crowd in the marketplace, not the agony of the madman, who held what was destroyed in awe and reverence. The new atheism does not think the subject worth a decent argument. In the old atheism, only the madman knew what had taken place. The crowd, nameless and strident, had simply accepted the impossibility of belief: "The greatest recent event," Nietzsche wrote, "that God is dead, that belief in the Christian god has become unbelievable—is already beginning to cast its first shadows over Europe." As those shadows lengthened over what had once been Christian faith, atheism became a more commonplace conviction.

This became not the heroic disbelief of the prophetic voices of the 19th century, but rather the bourgeois indifference to transcendence and the superficially secured contempt of the crowd. Feuerbach, [Karl] Marx, George Eliot, Nietzsche, Schopenhauer and [Sigmund] Freud yielded place to Sam Harris, Daniel Dennett, Peter Atkins and Richard Dawkins. It seems painfully obvious that the second string is of lesser caliber than the first; indeed, they should not besport themselves on the same field. Harsh but warranted is the judgment of the Oxford mathematician and author John Lennox: "On matters of theology, their arguments are a disgrace: assertion without substance, demanding evidence, while offering none, staggeringly unscholarly."

Lennox is not alone in discounting the attainments of the new atheism. The impoverished argument advanced by some recent atheist authors reveals, as perhaps nothing else, its weary and pervasive ignorance of what was regarded by their adversaries as "[w]hat was holiest and mightiest of all that the world has yet owned." If one stays with the parable of Nietzsche, the frame of the marketplace can remain the same. The new atheism has simply given recent and celebrated names to the faces in the crowd. They have become the crowd, but the superficiality and self-assurance remain.

Fairness and Respect Are Needed

Criticism of the new atheism cannot take up each one of its charges against religion and respond. The procedure of the new atheists has made such a reply impossible. What is lacking in the attacks is a fundamental evenhandedness and balance. The argument and discussion require a pervasive and fundamental presence of the liberal arts tradition, the grammar, rhetoric and logic that would discipline language and thought into reasoned conversations and arguments.

It is evident that recent attacks on religion do not issue from a profound knowledge of theology, history, philosophy and disciplined intellectual capacities. One will often look in vain for a cogent argument or a sober appeal to history. Even more disappointing is the ignorance of Christian fundamentals. In the *London Review of Books*, Terry Eagleton begins his review of Dawkins's *The God Delusion*: "Imagine someone holding forth on biology whose only knowledge of the subject is the *Book of British Birds*, and you have a rough idea of what it feels like to read Richard Dawkins on theology." What one comes across are "vulgar caricatures of religious faith that would make a first-year theology student wince."

Criticisms leveled at religion and at religious practices can be of immeasurable service to the purification of religion from pretense and facility, but what is one to do with this confused mass of imprecisions and travesties? One certainly cannot take the statements one by one, or the process would never end. Perhaps one should do nothing at all, insisting that real argumentation demands care, skill and honesty, and that the alternatives are a waste of time. But this is little more than cultural submission. Perhaps the best strategy is to adopt the procedures of the Mississippi River pilots: take soundings. Select a particular region on the fast-moving river, drop in a lead line to test out the depth and the shallows of the water, register the findings and compare them with the results of similar explorations. The knowledge gained could be of incomparable value in navigating the waters.

"Traditional religious moralists are apt to be authoritarian; they set great store in the traditional sacred cows, condone injustice, extol the wielders of power, and applaud the defenders of wealth and the status quo."

Atheism Teaches Morality and Ethics

Paul Kurtz

In the following viewpoint, Paul Kurtz contends that the morality of secular humanists is based on a belief that each person is responsible for his or her own destiny, as well as on the basic ideas of fairness and democracy and equal rights for all. He argues that traditional religious morality does not support civil rights for all and expects strict adherence to the religious beliefs that accompany that morality. Paul Kurtz is the editor in chief of Free Inquiry *and the Professor Emeritus of Philosophy at the State University of New York at Buffalo.*

As you read, consider the following questions:

1. According to Paul Kurtz, why is the morality of secular humanism optimistic?

Paul Kurtz, "Two Competing Moralities: The Principles of Fairness contra 'Gott Mit Uns!'" *Free Inquiry*, vol. 24, June-July 2004, Copyright © 2004 Council for Democratic and Secular Humanism, Inc. This article originally appeared in Free Inquiry magazine. Reproduced by permission.

2. In Kurtz's opinion, which five questionable actions do extreme religious moralists support?

3. According to the author, how does the phrase "Gott mit uns" apply to the beliefs of the extreme religious moralists?

The cultural divide in America today cuts deep, separating two contending conceptions of morality. Those who believe that there is a need for a moral reformation based on the principles of fairness confront "evangelical foot soldiers" convinced that God is on their side (*"Gott mit uns!"*) in an all-out battle between good and evil.

The City of Humankind Versus That of God

The first form of morality is humanistic and secular. Its chief aim is to realize human happiness in "the city of humankind." It wishes to rely on reflective intelligence in resolving moral dilemmas. It emphasizes tolerance and the negotiation of differences. It holds that men and women are responsible for their own destinies and that they can, with some measure of goodwill, achieve meaningful and enriched lives for themselves and their communities. It advocates the civic virtues of democracy and the extension of universal human rights to all persons on the planet.

The second form of morality is traditional religious morality, which has taken on an extremist evangelical and fundamentalist twist in recent years. It is focused on the "City of God" and the coming, apocalyptic end of civilization as we know it. Rooted in religious faith, allegedly revealed to our forebears who lived in a nomadic and agricultural culture of the past, it declares that humans are "sinful" and that their ultimate duty is to obey the moral commandments, divinely delivered. Since we are dependent upon God for salvation, human beings in themselves are incapable of achieving moral virtue. There are absolute commandments that a person must believe in and follow. Evangelical doomsday prophets today declare that the end times are approaching. They view the wars in the Middle East as signs of divine deliverance. Those who believe in Jesus as their savior will be saved by the divine Rapture, those who do not will be, as in Tim LaHaye and Jerry Jenkins's best-selling novels, *Left Behind* to suffer terrible punishment.

Secular humanists are skeptical of this apocalyptic interpretation of human history and cosmic destiny. It would be difficult to take this dramatic tale seriously, if not for the fact that it is taken so seriously by tens of millions of well-meaning Americans who hold considerable political and economic power. Secular humanists turn instead to modern science for their interpretation of the cosmos and the place of the human species within it. Science explains the emergence of the human species as a product of evolution; it seeks to explain the universe in natural, causal terms. Secular humanists' moral outlook is not weighed down by anthropocentric concepts of sin, guilt, redemption, and salvation. It is optimistic about the potentialities for improving the human condition.

Fortunately, many liberal religionists are equally disturbed by fundamentalist doomsday prophecies, and they are sympathetic to the principles and values of humanist morality. Although they are surely influenced by the Old and New Testaments, they tend to interpret Scripture in nonliteral terms. They realize the complexities of decision-making and are less doctrinaire in their approach to the moral life. Humanists hold that there are widely shared moral virtues (the common moral decencies) and also basic values (the ethical excellences) that both religious and nonreligious people respect. Humanists and liberal believers share a commitment to tolerance and the civic virtues of democracy. They agree that there are universal human rights, though these are not to be found in the

Bible. And they are dubious of intransigent religious absolutes. They agree that religious piety by itself is no substitute for using human intelligence, fallible as it may be, to solve moral problems. Both humanists and liberal believers wish to apply modern science for the betterment of the human condition. Unfortunately, their views are often drowned out by loud evangelical-fundamentalist voices.

The dispute between extremist religious moralists (orthodox and fundamentalist) on the one side and secular humanists and liberal religionists on the other takes many forms today. Extremist religious moralists consider America to be "one nation under God" (they equate patriotism with religious faith). Both secular and religious liberals fear theocracies; they cherish the First Amendment and the separation of church and state.

Extremist religious moralists oppose abortion, euthanasia, contraception, and women's rights. They consider homosexuality sinful. They are all too often xenophobic [afraid of foreigners] about the rest of the world. They object to any questioning of their absolute certainties, whether from science, reason, humanism, democracy, the United Nations, or the World Court. Secular humanists believe in individual freedom, the right of privacy, and the building of a world community—convictions that, fortunately, most religious liberals share.

The Violation of a Basic Human Right

One issue caught in today's cultural divide is same-sex marriage. Some conservative religious moralists seek to enact a constitutional amendment that would prohibit it. They insist that marriage must be between one man and one woman, as is divinely sanctified by the Bible; further, they believe that heterosexual marriage is threatened by gay marriage.

This dispute over marriage is rather puzzling, since religious denominations often disagree vehemently about the institution. Conservative Roman Catholics oppose divorce under any circumstances (although not annulments), and they defend the unnatural state of celibacy; liberal Protestants, Jews, and religious humanists will allow divorce under certain conditions and are more receptive to sexual expression generally. Muslims also approve of divorce; in addition, they have sanctioned polygamy. Women are considered inferior to men and devoid of basic human rights in most parts of the Islamic world. Judaic-Christian religions have defended monogamy and are opposed to polygamy or bigamy. Yet the Old Testament condones patriarchy, concubinage, and polygamy: Abraham had many concubines and wives. Rachel bore Jacob no children, so she gave him her slave-girl Bilhah, who bore him sons. Jesus apparently never married and bade his disciples to leave their wives. Paul admonished wives to obey their husbands. So much for traditional biblical morality and its anti-family and anti-woman attitudes!

Secular humanists today would recognize marriages between two individuals, no matter what their gender. Mature adults should be permitted to work out their own living arrangements, and if they choose to join together should enjoy the same rights—economic, political, and social—as persons in religiously sanctified marriages. Liberal Episcopalians, Methodists, Jews, and Catholics empathize with this viewpoint. There is considerable evidence that homosexuality is genetic (for example, homosexual behavior is found in other species). Given this, civil society ought not to discriminate against same-sex preferences. The right of privacy between consenting adults is at stake. Nor should society fear the creation of new or extended marital forms. The reality of modern society is already that the nuclear family represents only a minority of households, and *de facto* [in practice] there is pluralistic diversity in relationships. Romantic affairs and a high divorce rate are omnipresent among heterosexuals. Partly in response to the AIDS epidemic, large numbers of gays have

abandoned promiscuity and have sought stable relationships—in defense of marital bonds, as it were.

Incidentally, I prefer the term *civil union* rather than *marriage* (though I would accept either), for what is at issue is
equal protection under the laws for all adult couples: equal
rights in property, taxation, inheritance, insurance, retirement,
health care, visitation rights, etc. *Homogamy* (same-sex unions)
seems to me to best describe the relationship of two individuals of the same sex, similar to *heterogamy* for heterosexuals. I
think that a constitutional amendment banning same-sex
marriage or civil unions would be an unfair violation of human rights.

Present state laws specifying who may marry are grossly
unfair to the nonreligious: secular humanists, atheists, and agnostics. States issue marriage licenses. However, the only offi-
ciants allowed to conduct a marriage ceremony are those au-
thorized by religious institutions or governmental officials (a
justice of the peace, judge, mayor, etc.). Regulations differ
state by state, but in the United States, approximately forty-
five states of the union offer no provision for couples to have
a binding public marriage ceremony officiated by a private
secular organization of their choice, such as a university, fra-
ternal organization, or humanist organization. I have conducted humanist wedding ceremonies for many couples, but
these are not legally recognized in New York State. To solem-
nize their vows in the eyes of the law, the couple must have
another wedding with a priest, minister, rabbi, or public official in attendance. This constitutes egregious discrimination.
European countries recognize civil ceremonies; why not the
United States? Public ceremonies performed by the Council
for Secular Humanism (which is an educational organization)
are not recognized in most states. The Church of Scientology,
Baptists, Jehovah's Witnesses, Mormons, Hindus, and Muslims
are recognized, but not secular institutions. Talk about unfair-
ness!

The Religious Want to Censor Science

A second area of contention today is the dispute regarding biogenetic research. Traditional religious moralists once opposed artificial insemination; yet millions of happy children and parents have benefited from these procedures. Today, they seek to ban cloning research of any kind, therapeutic or reproductive. This is not only short-sighted, but hypocritical. The same conservatives who oppose governmental regulation in the economy now clamor for it in science.

Leon Kass, chairman of the President's Council on Bioethics and a professed devotee of the Old Testament, vigorously opposes embryonic stem-cell research. That there should even be a presidential council in the first place is highly questionable, especially since this body, which is biased, has become the chief exponent of censorship. (Indeed, a dissident liberal member of this body was recently fired.) In an op-ed piece in the *Wall Street Journal* ("Reproduction and Responsibility," April 2004), Kass called for a series of "legislative moratoria" to prohibit various "new reproductive techniques." In particular, Kass wishes to ban any research on embryos older than ten to fourteen days. Presumably, he is reflecting the Roman Catholic doctrine of "ensoulment" that has recently been adopted by fundamentalist Protestants. If and when this legislation is brought to the Congress, it would exacerbate the cultural war; for traditional religious moralists believe this research on embryos is sinful; whereas secular humanists and their liberal religious allies wish to use science to improve the human condition. Such repressive policies could block efforts by biogenetic scientists to eliminate disease, reduce suffering, and extend life. Shades of the censorship of Galileo and Darwin!

Traditional religious moralists have often sought to block scientific progress on the basis of little more than fear of the unknown. In my view, any limits placed on research should come from within the scientific community, not from the pro-

Atheists Act Morally of Their Own Will

Fundamentalists do what they perceive as good deeds in order to fulfill God's will and to earn salvation; atheists do them simply because it is the right thing to do. Is this also not our most elementary experience of morality? When I do a good deed, I do so not with an eye toward gaining God's favor; I do it because if I did not, I could not look at myself in the mirror. A moral deed is by definition its own reward.

Slavoj Zizek, "Defenders of the Faith,"
New York Times, *March 12, 2006.*

tests of extreme religious moralists who are willing to use governmental power to bludgeon scientific inquiry.

Traditional Religious Morality Is Hypocritical

The double standard of traditional religious morality is apparent. I need hardly point out that the Vatican, which opposes same-sex marriage and cloning research as immoral, at the same time confronts a celibate priesthood, a significant minority of whose members have practiced pedophilia.

There are numerous actions and policies condoned by extreme religious moralists that secular humanists find abhorrent, especially those that violate the principles of fairness. I will mention some of them:

1. The demands for censorship of sexual displays are today prominent. Traditional religious moralists rail against Janet Jackson for having bared her breast during the Super Bowl, and they object to the use of vulgar exple-

tives by Howard Stern, but where are their criticisms of the excessive violence in television, radio, movies, and throughout the mass media?

2. Nor do traditional religious moralists criticize the resort to violence by state or federal governments. Capital punishment is opposed by many liberal humanists and religionists on moral grounds. Traditional religious moralists attempt to justify the death penalty by appeals to the Old Testament's principle of retribution. Susan Jacoby, in her new book *Freethinkers: A History of American Secularism* (2004), cites [Supreme Court Justice] Antonin Scalia in a 2002 speech: "Death is no big deal," he said, and then advocated the death penalty on constitutional and divine grounds. Virtually all of the European democracies have prohibited the death penalty. The World Court recently criticized the United States for sentencing fifty-one Mexican citizens to death without allowing them to consult their own embassy; capital punishment is illegal in Mexico.

3. Many religious traditionalists have defended preemptive wars, a policy deplored by many of America's friends and allies. Extremist religious moralists are all too eager to express self-righteous patriotic, nationalistic, and chauvinistic slogans in support of the use of military force.

4. Traditional religionists who loathe sexual transgressions have largely ignored greed and avarice. All too often, wealth is considered as synonymous with virtue (consider just two examples, Pat Robertson and John Templeton). Traditionalists carefully ignore the saying attributed to Jesus that it is rare for a rich man to enter into heaven. This corruption has spilled over into the political system, where campaign contributors and lob-

byists influence the legislative process, undermining environmental protection and other regulations essential for the common good.

5. Another point of contention—on moral grounds—is traditionalists' failure to show concern for the welfare of the disadvantaged, the poor, or even the middle class at the same time that the elephantine compensation of corporate executives is extolled. A basic principle of fairness in our democracy is at stake. The CEOs of the two hundred largest companies earned on average $9.2 million in salaries, bonuses, and stock options in 2003. (Of course, some received far more.) Although stock options granted were down from the previous year, cash payments to CEOs increased 14.4 percent, whereas the increase in the average worker's pay was only 2 percent. Moreover, in 2003 there was an increase in unemployment. In addition, the amount of taxes paid by corporations has steadily declined. From 1996 to 2000, 63 percent of U.S. corporations paid no corporate income tax at all, while 94 percent paid taxes equal to less than 5 percent of their net income. Traditionalists accept sharp disparities in income and wealth in America today, are willing to provide lower tax rates for capital gains and dividends as distinct from money earned from labor or work, and refuse to enact an increased minimum wage. All this is typical of their uncaring attitude. All of it fulfills, as I've argued before, the sacred principles of "evangelical capitalism." This is further illustrated by the continued decline of progressive income tax rates, the determined effort to repeal the estate tax entirely, and the amassing of large speculative fortunes in the stock market and real estate. In his disturbing book, *Wealth and Democracy* (2002), Kevin Phillips points out that the United States is well on its way to becoming an entrenched plutocracy [rule by the wealthy].

Values Have Shifted in Favor of Wealth

Get-rich schemes are in abundance. State-sponsored lotteries, *I Want to Be a Millionaire* game shows, and the building of gambling casinos illustrate the skewing of values. Gambling casinos are going up almost everywhere in the United States, no doubt in the hope that they will improve the local economies. Yet they often appear in depressed communities and attract the poorest sectors of society. The social and psychological costs of gambling, such as dependency, debt, domestic violence, family breakdowns, bankruptcy, and suicide and other deaths, is overlooked in the effort to advertise and promote casinos. I, of course, believe in a free market; however, I also believe that consumers should be warned about the pitfalls of slot machines—it is rare that anyone can make a fast buck, unless he or she stops after a big win.

I am surely not defending any form of Puritan repression but merely pointing out the distorted priorities of the traditional religious moralists. Bill Bennett was the czar of conservative morality in America, attempting to defend the old time religious morality, yet he lost a fortune in gambling and smoked like a fiend. What is the point? That one person's virtue becomes another's vice.

In defending the principles of fairness or social justice, I am not defending socialism, as one critic has characterized my criticism of evangelical capitalism. The term *socialism* referred to the nationalization of the means of production and/or the domination of the entire economy by the government. I believe in the vitality of the free-market capitalist system. What I am talking about is the application of simple moral principles of equity and fairness.

Secularists Are Concerned About All Human Beings

The two moralities that I've outlined above may be contrasted in the light of [American psychologist] Lawrence Kohlberg's stages of moral growth and development. Traditional religious moralists are apt to be authoritarian; they set great store in the traditional sacred cows, condone injustice, extol the wielders of power, and applaud the defenders of wealth and the status quo. In contrast, secular humanists have an altruistic concern for the happiness of all human beings within the planetary community. Liberal religious allies have common cause with secular humanists in the criticism of xenophobic, authoritarian nationalists.

Last but not least, America's growing legions of evangelical foot soldiers are now awaiting the Second Coming of Jesus and the Rapture, or so we are told by the best-selling authors of the *Left Behind* novels. They are convinced that God will save only their brand of evangelical Protestants (and perhaps those conservative Roman Catholics to the right of Attila the Hun). They will "leave behind" all others who do not accept their form of creedal fascism. Like the earlier defenders of the Aryan race, they insist that God agrees with them, and that all other Christian denominations, Jews, Muslims, Buddhists, Hindus, secular humanists, atheists, agnostics, and freethinkers—the bulk of humankind—will be condemned to hell. Unless you are prepared to believe in our way, say these true believers in our midst, you deserve to go to hell! This means that of the six billion people on the planet, only a relatively small number will enter the kingdom of heaven.

This attitude is similar to that of Islamic terrorists who insist that only those who accept the Qur'an as revealed by Muhammad will go to heaven—true believers who are prepared to detonate themselves and kill as many people as they can in the name of Allah. A new form of moral intolerance has descended on the world. *Gott mit uns* was a frightening paean to patriotism, intolerance, violence, and hatred sung by fascist storm troopers of another era as they marched off to "redeem" the world.

What will happen to love, compassion, and caring grace, extended to all humans in the community of humankind, no matter what their religious beliefs; what will happen to the common moral decencies and the principles of fairness and equity—if they get their way?

> *"Christian life calls us toward authentic love of God, neighbor and self and teaches us that we ought to fear sin and love God as our savior and redeemer."*

Only Religion Can Teach Morality and Ethics

Stephen J. Pope

In the following viewpoint, Stephen J. Pope contends that belief in God inspires individuals to strive for compassion. He rejects the arguments of atheists, that religion allows people to accept the word of God without question, by citing the disagreements by many Christians over the question of artificial contraception. Pope, a professor of theological ethics at Boston College, is the author of Human Evolution and Christian Ethics.

As you read, consider the following questions:

1. According to Stephen Pope, what kinds of social issues of "moral absolutes" divide Christians?

2. According to the author, how is "human sin" the cause of evil?

3. In Pope's opinion, what are the four forms of altruism?

Who are the "new atheists"? Broadly speaking, they are a collection of writers who have come together in recent years in their disdain for the very idea of God. They regard religion as the last bastion of superstition, obscurantism, and fear and see the Christian churches as dedicated to inhibiting progress and human freedom. They regard biological evolution as providing the best overall account of who we are, where we have come from and where we might go as a species.

Religion "poisons everything," proclaims the journalist Christopher Hitchens, and religious morality amounts to psychological abuse. The sociobiologist Richard Dawkins describes religion as a "virus," and in *The God Delusion* proclaims that monotheism is "the great unmentionable evil at the center of our culture." Dawkins regards theistic ethics as commanding obedience to a biblical God whose jealous and violent character is anything but morally admirable. The philosopher Daniel Dennett depicts religion as a willful attempt to pass on ignorance through promises that can never be kept. He asserts that religious morality based on sacred texts immunizes people from asking critical questions. And in *The End of Faith*, Sam Harris argues that faith only generates "solidarity born of tribal and tribalizing fictions." Its promotion of irrationality dangerously sanctions a habit of acting out of religious conviction unrestrained by humility or compassion.

One can certainly raise questions about the accusations of the new atheism, but practical constraints narrow my focus to three issues: first, the relation between belief in God and morality; second, the relation between morality, reason and religion; and third, the relation between morality and the Christian ethic of love. The new atheist critique of Christian morality usually applies (if at all) only to a fundamentalist minority of Christians. Yet because this literature hits home with many readers, we Christians have to take seriously both its criticisms and our responsibility to present a better public witness to the truth of the Gospel.

Belief in God Helps Us to Be Moral

Much of the new atheist literature is reactive in that it begins by sharply criticizing what it rejects. The new atheists react against a triple claim often advanced by religious people: that belief in a personal God is necessary for people to have moral knowledge, for people to do what is right and avoid wrong, and for people to justify moral absolutes.

First, some Christians claim that belief in a God who reveals the divine law presents the sole (or most reliable) basis for knowing right from wrong. Reason takes people all over the place, but only religious authority can settle things once and for all. Yet the value of a given moral authority does not prove either its legitimacy or reliability. Such an approach to moral security is made the more troublesome by the fact that Christians who rely on the same scriptural authority, as well as Catholic Christians who profess loyalty to a single hierarchy, often disagree on moral issues. Belief in God does not exempt one from the difficult work of interpreting the significance of specific biblical texts or church teachings for our own day. On the contrary, it can make moral reasoning at least as complex as anything one finds in texts of moral philosophy.

The Catholic tradition walks a middle way between the religious positivist, who says we ought to rely only on religious authority, and the new atheist, who claims reason to be self-sufficient. Catholics affirm the need for community and the value of the accumulated wisdom of the past; Catholics also hold that each person is created with a conscience and has access to the natural law through the exercise of his or her moral intelligence. God teaches us through the exercise of our reason within the church and the broader social world within which we act.

Second, some Christians assert that belief in God supplies a necessary motive for doing right and avoiding wrong. The so-called sanction argument holds that fear of divine wrath keeps people on the narrow path; without it people are capable of anything. The new atheists properly target those who take this deeply pessimistic view of the human person, curbed from evil only by threat of eternal punishment. As Harris puts it, our "common humanity is reason enough to protect our fellow human beings from coming to harm."

On this point, Catholic moral anthropology is closer to the new atheists than to Christian fear-mongers. It regards each person's conscience as capable of being moved by an innate "connaturality" with the good. God does not inspire in us a servile fear, which, as [philosopher] David Hume noted long ago, is an essentially egocentric position. Rather, Christian life calls us toward authentic love of God, neighbor and self and teaches us that we ought to fear sin and love God as our savior and redeemer.

Third, the new atheists reject the claim that only belief in God provides the basis for exceptionless moral prohibitions. Harris regards moral absolutism as proposing a "certainty without evidence" that "is necessarily divisive and dehumanizing." Even Christian critics see the question-begging nature of an apologetic tack that takes for granted the legitimacy of moral absolutes. It also ignores the fact that some atheists display a very strong moral code, justified by reasons independent of belief in God. The new atheists recognize the wrongfulness of murder, rape and the like. Yet one might argue that this thin concession does not provide a sufficiently detailed ethic regarding morally complex and contentious cases, especially concerning the most vulnerable among us. Moral absolutes against abortion, embryonic stem cell research and physician-assisted suicide can be maintained, Christians might argue, only by reliance on divinely mandated or church-endorsed morality.

Yet the fact that Christians themselves are sharply divided over the ethics of life indicates that belief in God does not necessarily guarantee consensus over the content of particular moral absolutes. The significant gap between the small minority of Christians who accept the absolute prohibition on artificial contraception and the vast majority who differentiate between its proper and improper uses illustrates this point. The Catholic natural law tradition does not teach that we come to know the strictly binding character of these norms only through divine revelation or ecclesial instruction. It affirms that one can attain knowledge of moral norms through the use of human moral intelligence.

Violence Has Also Been Committed in the Name of Reason

A major issue raised by the new atheists concerns the relation between Christian morality and reason. The new atheists want us to reject Christianity for the sake of moral progress, then to draw an antinomy between two massive domains of human agency—reason and religion—in order to promote the dominance of the former and the destruction of the latter. At times they concede that the Christian tradition has made some important historical contributions to human well-being (including universities and hospitals), but they argue that everything good in the Christian tradition is because of the operation of reason within it. Conversely, everything bad in the tradition is because of religion, not reason. This line of argumentation is arbitrary, tendentious [showing a definite bias] and viciously circular. It ignores the fact that the global (and ill-defined) categories of "reason" and "religion" are not alternatives but rather two forms of human activity that can be related variously: competitively, cooperatively or in other ways. From a Christian standpoint, the cause of evil can be attributed neither to religion nor reason, but to human sin—the

Our Rights Were Given to Us by God

They [the Founding Fathers] founded a nation on the revolutionary notion that man's rights are granted by God and government derives its power from the consent of those it governs. If there is no God then from where do we obtain inalienable rights? And without these natural rights, the purpose of government cannot be to secure them for individual men.

Joseph C. Phillips, "God and Civics,"
Chicago Defender, *December 21–23, 2007.*

willful decision to put what is essentially good to evil uses out of greed, pride or other twisted motivations.

There is no question that sometimes evildoing has been pursued under the guise of religion, but the same can be said of science. The new atheists display their innocence of the complexity of historical causation when they simply point to "religion" as the prime cause of the wrongdoing of Christians, ranging from Augustine's defense of using violence to repress heretics to the "silence" of Pius XII during the Holocaust. One could just as easily (and cheaply) blame reason for similar horrors. If the Nazis had not been so intelligently organized, they could not have managed their factories of death so efficiently. I say this facetiously, but the writings of the new atheists are replete with such simpleminded rhetoric from self-appointed champions of reason.

Christian Ethics Include Love and Compassion

Some of the new atheists, informed by sociobiology and evolutionary psychology, hold that Christian morality proposes an impossibly high norm of love; meanwhile, the actual conduct of Christians tends to conform to neo-Darwinian expectations that we care for "our own" and not others. In their view, what we need is a more realistic ethic, less lofty but more effective.

Dawkins regards morality as a set of normative standards that rewards good acts with social approval and punishes bad acts with social disapproval, and within which an individual promotes his or her evolutionary self-interest through morality. Altruism typically takes one of four forms: "kin altruism" toward relatives and especially our own children; "reciprocal altruism," which trades benefits with friends in mutually beneficial relationships; generous acts, which accrue "reputational benefits"; and acts of assistance, which enhance an individual's own social status. In every society, morality promotes individual conformity to socially agreed-upon patterns of reciprocity that allow communities to function with some degree of order, regularity and peace. Christian morality does the same.

The new atheists regard Christian love as a completely unrealistic form of altruism. Despite high-flown sentiments, most Christians channel their resources to their own loved ones rather than to the poor. A small degree of altruism can be taught by culture, but instructing human beings to be altruistic is, to use Dawkins's metaphor, like training a bear to ride a unicycle. Altruism toward a stranger is an "evolutionary mistake," and those who regularly practice indiscriminate altruism can expect to be evolutionary failures as well as impoverished.

Advocates of Christian morality can respond to this position in several ways.

First, it is important to admit that the actual conduct of Christians often leaves a great deal to be desired. In-group favoritism and out-group oppression, sometimes against one another's subgroups and more often against outsiders, can do more damage to the Christian community than any new atheist tract ever could. The new atheists echo Freud's denunciation of the contradiction between the universal ethic of the Gospel and the history of Christian brutality toward the Jews.

Second, the new atheists' moral critique replicates the Christian tradition's own internal criticisms of religious hypocrisy, apathy and self-deception. The prophetic tradition, for example, launched its sharpest criticisms against those who practiced liturgical correctness while being indifferent to the suffering of the poor. And it is clear that we have yet to grasp fully the implications of Jesus' mission to save sinners, not the righteous. Christian prophets have recognized, as Dorothy Day once observed, that the Christian must live in a state of "permanent dissatisfaction with the church."

Third, the critique applies to sectarian Christians who suggest that the Christian ethic constitutes a completely radical way of life that transcends all normal human needs and limitations and to those who interpret discipleship as an ethic for saints and heroes, but not for ordinary people. Yet Catholic ethics regards grace as the perfection of human nature, not its enemy. The church acknowledges that divine grace enables people like Oscar Romero [a bishop of the Roman Catholic Church in El Salvador] to lead heroically self-giving lives. The church also understands that grace calls most of us to follow the Gospel in everyday life as we take care of our families, friends, and neighbors. Even the most demanding Christian ideals, such as the preferential option for the poor, are sustained when they are pursued within life-giving personal relationships and communities.

Acts of Compassion Mean More than Reason

The anti-religious polemics offered by the new atheists are often unfair, uninformed and hysterical. Yet their body of work offers us a salutary reminder of the importance of two dimensions of moral integrity: the intellectual and the practical. Christian ethics is based on the belief that the purpose of human existence is neither the "replication of genes" nor the "survival of the fittest," but the development of our capacity to understand and to love.

The new atheists rightly complain about the unreflective and ill-informed nature of much Christian belief. Harris laments, for example, the pervasive superficiality and anti-intellectualism of popular Christianity; Dawkins criticizes the "distressingly little curiosity" that religious people show regarding their own faith. It is no consolation that secular people in our society display similar weaknesses. While the attacks of the new atheists reveal their ignorance of the Christian faith, their call for greater intellectual honesty within the Christian community is appropriate and ought to be heeded.

The new atheists also consistently point to a gap between Christian beliefs and Christian conduct. But if the flawed conduct adds fuel to the new atheists' fire, does not the highest Christian witness snuff out at least some of the flames? Beliefs begin to make sense only when they are embodied in real lives. True Christians exemplify the love of God and neighbor in everyday life in work, family and community life; and the examples of Christians who selflessly serve the poor and neglected are worth more than 1,000 books on moral theology.

For most of us, belief or unbelief has little to do with proofs for God's existence or the intellectual cogency of Trinitarian theology. Most people are attracted (or repelled) by the quality of the lives of the individual Christians they encounter, rather than by the intellectual appeal of Christian beliefs. The primary response of Christians to the new atheism, then, should not be to marshal better moral counterarguments, but to engage in concrete actions that show that Christian beliefs are not sentimental illusions. As the author of 1 John put it, "let us love not with word or with tongue but in deed and in truth" (3:18).

Periodical Bibliography

The following articles have been selected to supplement the diverse views presented in this chapter.

Jennifer Bardi — "Stark's Reason: How a California Congressman Became the Most Honest Person in Politics," *The Humanist*, May-June 2007.

Joseph Chuman — "The Role of Religion on Belief and Behavior," *Bergen County Record*, May 14, 2007.

E.J. Dionne Jr. — "Answer to the Atheists," *Washington Post*, April 6, 2007.

Michael Gerson — "What Atheists Can't Answer," *Washington Post*, July 13, 2007.

Christopher Hitchens — "An Atheist Responds," *Washington Post*, July 14, 2007.

David Hodgson — "Dawkins and the Morality of the Bible," *Quadrant*, May 2007.

Jeff Jacoby — "Why We Need Religion," *Boston Globe*, April 18, 2007.

Joyce McMillan — "Myth of Creationism Weakens the Vital Morality of Religion," *The Scotsman*, September 13, 2008.

Michael and Jane Novak — "What Washington Saw in God: And How That Vision Shaped His Life and Presidency," *USA Today*, February 19, 2007.

Jim Wallis — "A Conversation on Moral Issues," *Sojourners Magazine*, May 2007.

OPPOSING VIEWPOINTS® SERIES

CHAPTER 3

What Are the Major Concerns of Atheism?

Chapter Preface

Ruling in two different cases over the public display of the Ten Commandments in 2005, the U.S. Supreme Court demonstrated the difficulty in drawing the line separating church and state. What some see as an expression of religious freedom, others see as forcing religion into public life.

In *Van Orden v. Perry*, the Court determined that a monument displaying the Ten Commandments outside a state capitol building in Texas did not violate the establishment clause of the First Amendment, which has been interpreted to mean that the federal government cannot declare or support a national religion or show preference to any religion. In *McCreary County v. ACLU of Kentucky*, however, the Court found that it was unconstitutional to display the Ten Commandments inside a courthouse.

Both cases were decided by five to four votes. In each case, the same four justices upheld the displays and the same four justices voted to invalidate the displays; only Justice Stephen Breyer voted differently in the two cases. According to the Web site of Duke University Law School, "In determining whether a particular display is a symbolic endorsement of religion, courts must look at its history, its purpose, and its context." From a historical standpoint, Justice Breyer observed that the display of the Ten Commandments in Kentucky had only recently been erected, while the monument in Texas had been on exhibit for forty years. He also believed that the purpose of the Ten Commandments display in Kentucky was distinctly religious, whereas that in Texas represented the notion of the Ten Commandments as the legal basis for society and, therefore, served a secular purpose. With regard to context, Breyer observed that the monument in Texas was just one of more than twenty other monuments on the grounds of the state capitol; in the Kentucky courthouse, however, Breyer took into consideration that additional elements of the exhibit had been chosen for their religious subject matter.

Those who believe that religion should play an integral role in government and society cite the importance of displaying the Ten Commandments publicly to help inspire and encourage morality. The American Center for Law & Justice notes that "There is a growing desire to display the Ten Commandments in all public venues because they traditionally have represented a moral floor for acceptable behavior and served as an antecedent to obedience to law. . . . Use of the Ten Commandments for their civic and moral significance should be not only permissible, but indispensable in encouraging age-old maxims of good citizenship." Advocates of these displays are concerned that the importance of the Ten Commandments—and religion—in society has been minimized, resulting in a rise in unethical and immoral behavior. They argue that the public display of the Ten Commandments sets a positive tone for society.

Supporters of the idea of the separation between church and state argue that it is not the role of the government to impose the beliefs of any religion on the public. The American Civil Liberties Union (ACLU) explains the difference between constitutional and unconstitutional religious displays: "A Christian cross that is fully visible from a public sidewalk is constitutionally protected when placed in front of a church. But if that same cross were moved across the street and placed in front of city hall, it would violate the Constitution. The issue is *not* 'religion in the public square'—as the rhetoric misleadingly suggests—but whether the government should be deciding whose sacred texts and symbols should be placed on government property and whose should be rejected."

The debate over the extent to which religion should be included in society is longstanding and will continue indefinitely. Supporters argue that it was the goal of the Founding Fathers for religion to play a major role in all aspects of

American life. Detractors, including atheists, maintain that it is wrong to impose the religious views of some on society as a whole. The authors in the following chapter present a variety of viewpoints about the primary concerns of atheists, focusing on what role, if any, religion should play in society.

> "The Framing Generation instituted one of the most innovative aspects of the Constitution: a rule that denied any religious entity sovereign power, and thereby privatized religion."

There Should Be Separation of Church and State

Marci Hamilton

In the following viewpoint, Marci Hamilton argues that the U.S. Constitution was intended to keep church and state separate. She uses the Pledge Protection Act of 2004 as an example of an attempt to undermine the ability of the U.S. Supreme Court to oversee Congress by throwing more control to state courts. Hamilton contends that the Constitution was written with the belief that religious diversity must be protected and respected. Hamilton is a professor of public law at Benjamin N. Cardozo School of Law at Yeshiva University.

As you read, consider the following questions:

1. According to Marci Hamilton, why did the Ninth Circuit Court find that it is unconstitutional to insist that students recite "under God" in the Pledge of Allegiance?

Marci Hamilton, "The Pledge Protection Act: The Lunacy of Letting Only State Courts Interpret the First Amendment," Findlaw.com, September 23, 2004. Reproduced by permission.

2. From what sources was the U.S. Constitution created, according to the author?

3. In Hamilton's opinion, how would the Pledge Protection Act have weakened the U.S. system of checks and balances?

[In September of 2004] ... the House Judiciary Committee voted to send the Pledge Protection Act to the full House [of Representatives], which is likely to take it up ... The Act—a bill that has many cosponsors—would deprive all federal courts, even the Supreme Court, of jurisdiction to hear constitutional challenges to the "under God" Pledge of Allegiance. This is only the latest attempt by Congress to force a pluralist society into a one-size-fits-all set of beliefs. [The bill was passed on September 23, 2004, but the Senate took no action.]

This is a remarkable violation of the separation of powers and the Establishment Clause. If the Act were to become law— and if it were, itself, to be upheld as constitutional—*only* state courts would be able to hear constitutional challenges to the Pledge.

We would therefore have a 50-state collection of views as to what the Free Exercise Clause, and the Establishment Clause, mean in this context. And that would be constitutional lunacy. Moreover, we would have Congress making its actions that involve compelled speech and religious viewpoint unreviewable!

The Act Undercuts the U.S. Supreme Court

The Act was introduced as a response to two high-profile decisions in a case involving the Pledge.

First, there was the federal decision by the U.S. Court of Appeals for the Ninth Circuit in *Newdow v. Elk Grove United School District*. There, the Ninth Circuit held that it is unconstitutional to require students to recite the phrase "under God" in the Pledge of Allegiance. This requirement, the Ninth Circuit reasoned, violates the Establishment Clause [which prevents the establishment of a national religion].

The Act may also have arisen from Congressional disappointment with the United States Supreme Court's ruling in *Newdow*. Rather than reaching the Establishment Clause issue, the Court held the plaintiff lacked standing—that is, the legal right—to bring the challenge.

The Supreme Court's ruling opened the way for another possible challenge to the "under God" pledge—one that, with a plaintiff who *did* have standing—could go all the way to the Supreme Court on the merits.

That, of course, is as it should be. The U.S. Supreme Court is properly the ultimate forum for questions concerning the interpretation of the U.S. Constitution. But the new Act would cut off that proper, time-honored path—and, as I have noted, it would leave Pledge issues to the state courts alone.

Taking Public Support to an Extreme

The reason the Act is moving through Congress now is no mystery. Various polls showed that a majority of the American public believed that the phrase "under God" should stay in the Pledge of Allegiance. So now, in an election year [2004], politicians are pandering to their constituents by supporting a bill that they can spin as one that would protect the Pledge.

Congress's actions are appalling. Of course, polls do not determine what laws should be laws. Far from it. Our elected representatives are supposed to be acting in the public good and according to constitutional principles, not led around by polling numbers. And if members of Congress looked to their constituents' deeper beliefs about the freedom of conscience and the freedom of speech, and to the good of the country, they would strongly oppose the Pledge Protection Act. There should be memorable oratory fighting this latest attempt to impose popular views on every American.

Americans do not support forcing children to choose between pledging allegiance to their country and being true to their religious beliefs. Nor do they support giving the government the power to force its citizens to recite any mantra, whether it is patriotic or not. The powers that be at the moment have covered over these fundamental beliefs with misleading blather about how this is a "Christian" nation, implying that Christians are the sole keeper of conscience and morals in the country.

The truth is, when forced to choose and not responding to some abstract polling question, Americans support the very freedoms our Constitution guarantees: The freedom to freely exercise one's religion, and the freedom from any religion established by the government. This is a country built on the freedom of conscience, a right that must be renewed by each subsequent generation.

Framers Believed in Religious Diversity

The Establishment Clause was motivated by the fear that Congress would oppress the American people in exactly the way Congress is now trying to do. It says that "Congress shall make no law respecting an establishment of religion. . . ." But by attempting to insulate the monotheistic "under God" Pledge from court review, in the Pledge Protection Act, that is exactly what Congress is trying to do. It's a one-God-fits-all formula that hearkens back to Britain under Queens Mary and Elizabeth who practiced the same principle, and only differed on which religion received their imprimatur [official approval].

From their own experiences in Britain and Europe, the Framing Generation knew the baleful consequences of joining the power of a national government with religion. The colonists came here in the wake of the Reformation and the extreme religious turbulence that resulted when Protestants and

The Constitution Limits Government, Not Religion

The separation of church and state does not mean the separation of God and government or of religion and politics. The First Amendment limits only the power of government—not the power of the people or of the church. Religious organizations are free to speak out on the issues of the day. They can preach, pray, proselytize, promote and, yes, even endorse candidates if they are foolish enough to do so.

Oliver "Buzz" Thomas, "So What Does the Constitution Say About Religion?" USA Today, October 15, 2007, p. A15.

Catholics jockeyed for power under the British monarchs. They knew, many of them firsthand, what happens when a centralized government becomes a partner with a particular religion.

This was why the Framing Generation instituted one of the most innovative aspects of the Constitution: a rule that denied any religious entity sovereign power, and thereby privatized religion. The result has been to make America a teeming, robust, and extraordinary marketplace in religion like the world has never seen.

The Framers also believed in the absolute freedom to believe whatever one wants—and therefore, they coupled the Establishment Clause with the Free Exercise Clause. They did not believe, of course, in an unfettered right to act, because actions can harm others, and the framing generation believed bad actions should be capable of being punished, regardless of the identity of the actor. But they believed religious practices ought to be left sacrosanct, as long as they stayed within the bounds of the duly enacted laws. They also believed in protecting, under the Constitution, a diversity of religious beliefs.

This is not a country that is based on any single religious vision—nor do we have a Constitution based on any single source, whether religious or secular. To the contrary, the Constitution was built on ideas taken from more than one Protestant theology, Roman and Greek government, and philosophers like [John] Locke, [Edmund] Burke, and [David] Hume. (The Framers also drew heavily on their experiences under the Articles of Confederation—when the country came very close to dissolving into 13 potentates, as opposed to a collection of states with common interests.)

Many of the Framers had rich classical educations—as did those with whom they corresponded. It is an insult to the Framers to reduce the sources from which they derived the Constitution to one aspect of some of their religious beliefs.

In sum, the House is not doing its homework if it believes that the government imposition of "under God" phrase reflects the views of the Framers. The country we have now is the one the Framers envisioned—one filled with religious believers of every stripe. It is an experiment they initiated that has had breathtaking success. Attempting to impose uniformity at this point through the "under God" Pledge betrays, rather than serves, the Framers' vision.

A System of Checks and Balances Is Needed

The Pledge Protection Act also betrays the Framers' vision in another way—it is a frontal attack on the valuable constitutional check provided by the federal judiciary.

The Framers, of course, believed in the absolute necessity of limiting power and pitting power against power so that no entity could get overweening power. Yet Congress is now attempting, with the Act, to deprive the federal courts of jurisdiction to check Congress's wayward ways—in an arena where Congress was specifically believed by the Framers to be dangerous. (Recall that phrase from the First Amendment's Establishment Clause, "Congress shall make no law . . .").

Do the members of Congress genuinely think that 50 state supreme courts—with a host of disparate views—could possibly keep Congress in check? Or do they perhaps, believe that as members of Congress, they need no check? My money is on the latter, but either way, they are very wrong.

Many Different Religions Are Practiced in the United States

There is no majority religion in the United States. No sect commands a majority of the United States population, though Protestants (which is in fact a category containing a collection of wildly differing beliefs) have formed a bare majority. However, that majority is slipping away year-by-year. Thus, it will not be long before the multiplicity of religions in this country will be such that Protestants are no longer a majority, and Protestantism is one among many other beliefs. That variety of beliefs fills the public square and fosters debate.

The fundamental disconnect in this entire debate was beautifully illustrated by former Alabama Judge Roy Moore's testimony before the House Judiciary Committee on an even more extreme bill stripping the federal courts of constitutional review. He said that current Establishment Clause doctrine "requires the complete removal of God from the public square." This is constitutional sleight of hand. The public square is that place where the many private voices in this society can be heard. The First Amendment exists to keep the government from intruding on that square, not to ensure the government—or a cabal of believers—dominates it.

In fact, after many years of federal judicial review of First Amendment issues, the public square is filled with a wide array of voices, including many religious voices, like Moore's. What Moore and those behind this embarrassing bill are chafing against is the fact they cannot use the government's power to back up their religious views.

They can hardly succeed in arguing that their views are excluded from the culture. If they are not influencing Congress to enact this crazy law, who is?

A number of religious organizations are admirably fighting this bill. Other religious interests should not squander their moral authority in an attempt to achieve political ends that are inimical to the Constitution and freedom. The Pledge Protection Act is just such an attempt. It is doomed to fail in the courts (for federal courts—least of all the Supreme Court—cannot be stripped of jurisdiction this way). Yet it also signals a larger failure on the part of institutions and persons who should be upholding our system, not trying to undermine it. This is not the time to abandon liberty.

"Religion was not something the founders necessarily feared and wanted distanced from society and government, but one that must be closely held and carefully regulated for the health of both society and government."

There Should Be No Separation of Church and State

Warner Todd Huston

In the following viewpoint, Warner Todd Huston contends that the Founding Fathers believed that religion must play an essential role in both government and society. He argues that the writings of Thomas Jefferson, James Madison, and others state very clearly that religion helps to maintain a just and civil society. Huston asserts that secularists have misinterpreted Jefferson's words, "separation of church and state," to mean that religion has no place in society or government. Warner Todd Huston owns and operates the Publius' Forum Web site, which publishes editorials and news stories about current events.

Warner Todd Huston, "Does 'Separation of Church and State' Really Exist?" Renewamerica.us, July 23, 2006. © Copyright 2006 by Warner Todd Huston. Reproduced by permission of the author.

As you read, consider the following questions:

1. According to Warner Todd Huston, what would a true reading of Thomas Jefferson's Danbury letter reveal about the states and religion?
2. According to the author, on which document is Justice Joseph Story considered to be an authority?
3. What did Justice Story write about government involvement with religious issues?

Secularists today have a catch phrase that they use like a club against religion in America. That club is named "The Separation of Church and State."

So many Americans have heard the phrase that they think it is one actually written right into the Constitution of the United States. Those who are more learned on the subject realize it is not. In fact, those who are learned on the subject know that it wasn't mentioned in any law, or even in the halls of Congress, until long after the Constitution was written. In fact, there was not much attention paid to the phrase at all until after Thomas Jefferson, the originator of the phrase, was long dead.

Not even the Supreme Court paid it much attention until the 1940s, so this "wall of separation" issue is not one that hails from the early Republic with the same meaning as it does today. Our Founders had very different ideas about religion and government, ideas that were not nearly as simple as the stark black or white assumptions of the activists of today.

A Misinformed Secular Presumption

The man who initially wrote the phrase, Thomas Jefferson, wrote it in an 1802 letter to a congregation of Baptist churchmen from Danbury, Connecticut. Only elected president of the United States but two years previously (1800–1808), Jefferson was responding to a letter sent him by the Danbury church members who were attempting to get his support for their struggle against the state's somewhat oppressive religious requirements for certain rights in that state—not an unusual practice in the states at that time. While Jefferson's letter only obliquely addressed the Baptists' concerns, more importantly it addressed the Federal position on establishing a national religion because Jefferson's reply was focused on the Federal issue, not that of the states.

In his short letter, Jefferson said, ". . . I contemplate with sovereign reverence that act of the whole American people which declared that their legislature should 'make no law respecting an establishment of religion, or prohibiting the free exercise thereof,' thus building a wall of separation between Church and State. Adhering to this expression of the supreme will of the nation in behalf of the rights of conscience. . . ."

Jefferson used the words "act of the whole American people" and "supreme will of the nation" for a very specific reason. While he obliquely seemed to be supportive of the Baptist's plight, he did not give them direct support for overturning Connecticut's state laws just on his say-so. Jefferson restricted his response to the Federal (or National) position, distancing himself from being seen to talk badly about the state's laws. After all, as president of the United States, Jefferson had no power to alter a state's Constitution. Worse, should a letter he had written attacking a state's Constitution on an issue that was commonly extant in most of the Union become public, it could lead to a messy backlash that Jefferson did not need after the tumultuous and vicious presidential campaign of 1800.

Lastly, it should be remembered that Jefferson already had an unsavory reputation as an irreligious heathen as the charge was leveled against him during the contentious 1800 campaign. Jefferson knew that every state in the Union (except Rhode Island) had a state sponsored religion since before the days of the Revolution, so by relegating himself to the settled national issue, he could not easily be accused of more atheist sentiments.

So, what does this mean to the issue of "separation of church and state" for today's argument? It means that Jefferson's letter should not be used by anti-religionists to support their position. Jefferson was clearly saying that religious issues were in the various states' area of influence and control, not his as leader of the Federal Union. Unfortunately, today's anti-religionists who wish to eliminate religion in the states as well as the Federal Union illegitimately use Jefferson's words in their cause, misconstruing Jefferson to say that all religion should be eliminated from government.

A true reading of Jefferson's letter would tend to undermine the secularists who imagine that Jefferson was saying in the Danbury letter that *all* government should be separated from religion because he made no effort to say that the states should emulate the Federal government's separation. After all, an "act of the whole American people" refers to those acts made concerning rules for the Federal Union, not those of the individual states.

In summation, Jefferson was addressing the separation of powers as much as he was that of the Federal government and religion.

Jefferson's Danbury letter, of course, was just one man's opinion and, to be sure, it was one made more to get someone off his back with a short address than one of any detailed discussion of the issue. But he was far from the only Founder to have considered the issue of religion, society, and the state.

Christianity Is the Foundation for Society

Their own personal religious practices aside, the Founders had an intense desire to see religion observed by the people, but where the Founder's brilliance lay was in an insistence for freedom of religious expression, not in a squelching of same.

James Madison, who addressed that subject many times, wrote that, "Among the features peculiar to the political system of the United States, is the perfect equality of rights which it secures to every religious sect."

Of course, Madison was quite explicit in his thoughts that government should not operate or directly run a religion, yet he was equally as insistent that religious observance was a very important aspect of republicanism. To expect that the same man who would say such things would advocate a total elimination of public religion just doesn't logically follow.

The Founders were as worried about virtue in the people as they were for their liberty and freedom, as it turns out. Here are just a few more quotes as grist for the mill for discussion.

Benjamin Rush:

> I proceed ... to enquire what mode of education we shall adopt so as to secure to the state all the advantages that are to be derived from the proper instruction of youth; and here I beg leave to remark, that the only foundation for a useful education in a republic is to be laid in religion. Without this there can be no virtue, and without virtue there can be no liberty, and liberty is the object and life of all republican governments.

George Washington:

> Whatever may be conceded to the influence of refined education on minds of peculiar structure, reason and experience both forbid us to expect that National morality can prevail in exclusion of religious principle.

And one more from James Madison:

> "The belief in a God All Powerful wise and good, is so essential to the moral order of the world and to the happiness of man, that arguments which enforce it cannot be drawn from too many sources nor adapted with too much solicitude to the different characters and capacities impressed with it."

With these few quotes (and there are many, many others) we see that the Founders desired the people to be led by religion. And, to be sure, the religion they assumed would play a leading role were the various forms of Christianity as existing in the Union at the time. So, we can easily establish that the Founders weren't anti-religion, that they desired religions to be included in American life, and that Christianity served as a necessary foundation upon which to build a civil society.

But what did it all really mean for the Constitution? For a fuller discussion of the issue we can turn to Supreme Court Associate Justice Joseph Story's writings.

Story's Writings Are Authoritative

Justice Story was born in 1779 and became an Associate Justice of the Supreme Court in 1811 after having previously been a distinguished politician from Massachusetts. He figured prominently later in the era of the John Marshall Court as the Supreme Court solidified its position as presumed final arbiter of Constitutionality of laws passed by Congress.

One of the things he is remembered for the most by posterity is his exposition on the Constitution. Story's *Commentaries on the Constitution of the United States* is still widely looked upon as the standard treatise on the subject of the Constitution of the United States. This treatment has been standard reading for law students, Constitutional historians, and students of civil government for 173 years and has served as a chief reference in some of the best schools for generations. There is no question that Story's work is considered authoritative and widely accepted.

It should be noted that Story's able commentaries on the Constitution were published in 1833 and were used as an authoritative textbook for study of the law and the Constitution all the way until our own times. As a measuring stick, it should be noted that the last of the Founders, James Madison, wouldn't pass away until 1836, three years after the publishing

Religion Cannot Be Separated from the State

The founders did not declare independence from England because they wanted to set up a secular state. They declared independence because of a long train of abuses and usurpations of government power against its people. They were concerned about matters of tyranny, not theology. The Boston Tea Party was about taxes (and thus enshrined in American tradition the fine art of complaining about taxes), not about Baptists throwing Presbyterians' Bibles into the Atlantic.

John Bambenek, "What Does Separation of Church and State Really Mean?" Liberty Magazine, October 31, 2007.

of Story's work. So, Story's era was still intimately connected to that of those who framed the Constitution. Story's commentaries were not viewed as revolutionary, or radical in any way.

Religion Is Needed for a Just Society

Congress shall make no law respecting an establishment of religion, or prohibiting the free exercise thereof; or abridging the freedom of speech, or of the press; or the right of the people peaceably to assemble, and to petition the Government for a redress of grievances [First Amendment to the Constitution].

To set the stage, we must first ascertain what Mr. Story and the Founders before him envisioned the role of religion in society, as well as in government, should be. We must review more than their thoughts on the place of religion and the Constitution to get an informed idea of what the Founders desired. Should we concern ourselves solely with their thoughts on religion and the Federal Constitution we give ourselves an incomplete picture of their thoughts on the matter and this tends to horribly skew the debate in too simplistic a direction.

That in mind we find that Justice Story went on at great length about the place of religion in government arriving at a point far from saying religion had no right or place to intermingle with government.

In one of his first few paragraphs on the First Amendment and the religion clause therein, Story said, "Indeed, the right of a society or government to interfere in matters of religion will hardly be contested by any persons, who believe that piety, religion, and morality are intimately connected with the well being of the state, and indispensable to the administration of civil justice."

This straightforward paragraph reveals that Story was hardly a man who imagined government and religion should be alienated one from the other! Story began with the basic assumption that the Christian religion was indispensable to a good society, echoing the thoughts of the Founders.

> ... the great doctrines of religion, the being, and attributes, and providence of one Almighty God; the responsibility to him for all our actions, founded upon moral freedom and accountability; a future state of rewards and punishments; the cultivation of all the personal, social, and benevolent virtues;—these never can be a matter of indifference in any well ordered community. It is, indeed, difficult to conceive, how any civilized society can well exist without them. And at all events, it is impossible for those, who believe in the truth of Christianity, as a divine revelation, to doubt, that it is the especial duty of government to foster, and encourage it among all the citizens and subjects. This is a point wholly distinct from that of the right of private judgment in matters of religion, and of the freedom of public worship according to the dictates of one's conscience.

After setting this basic groundwork, Story went on a brief review of the history of religion in the colonies and young states as it directly affects the Constitution and the American system—turning to history as the authors of the Federalist Papers did in their own exposition on the Constitution.

A History of State-Sponsored Religion

In so doing, he observes that every state had a state sponsored religion.

> In fact, every American colony, from its foundation down to the revolution, with the exception of Rhode Island, (if, indeed, that state be an exception,) did openly, by the whole course of its laws and institutions, support and sustain, in some form, the Christian religion; and almost invariably gave a peculiar sanction to some of its fundamental doctrines. And this has continued to be the case in some of the states down to the present period, without the slightest suspicion, that it was against the principles of public law, or republican liberty.

This all led Story to the conclusion that Christianity was never imagined to be detrimental to the health of the state or Federal government.

> Probably at the time of the adoption of the constitution, and of the amendment to it, now under consideration, the general, if not the universal, sentiment in America was, that Christianity ought to receive encouragement from the state, so far as was not incompatible with the private rights of conscience, and the freedom of religious worship. An attempt to level all religions, and to make it a matter of state policy to hold all in utter indifference, would have created universal disapprobation, if not universal indignation.

Story was not insensible to religious oppression, of course, and his next several sections dealt with the religious oppressions of western history up to the time of the Founding of the country. Again, history was his guide.

With his historical investigations revealing the all too common religious oppressions by past governments concluded, Story assured his readers that the issue of religion belonged properly with the states where the people had the most ability to affect it—as did the Founders before him.

> Thus, the whole power over the subject of religion is left exclusively to the state governments, to be acted upon according to their own sense of justice, and the state constitutions . . .

Religious Freedom Is Not the Same as Freedom from Religion

In the final analysis, Story observed no stark separation of church and state, but a practice of delegating a regulation of religion that rested with the various states. There was no expectation by the Founders or any language placed in the Constitution whereby religion would be banished from the public sphere. So this mythical "wall of separation" does not really exist but in the minds of later day anti-religionists.

The reality of the Founder's intent for the roles of government and religion were far more nuanced and complicated than modern religion banners pretend. Unfortunately, they are presenting an incorrect picture of history and Constitutional law that is damaging the system that the Founders created and materially altering our culture for the worse.

In closing, I'd like to quote one more Founder, Elias Boudinot, delegate from New Jersey to the Continental Congress from 1777 to 1778, and 1781 to 1784. Then President of the Continental Congress, 1783.

> Our country should be preserved from the dreadful evil of becoming enemies to the religion of the Gospel, which I have no doubt, but would be the introduction of the dissolution of government and the bonds of civil society.

Religion was not something the Founders necessarily feared and wanted distanced from society and government, but one that must be closely held and carefully regulated for the health of both society and government.

Unfortunately, anti-religionists today forget that our nation was based on and intimately connected with religious freedom. Not freedom from religion.

"It's undeniable that religion is powerful and it's undeniable that it's something that we, for perfectly pragmatic political reasons, need to know something about."

There Should Be Prayer and Bible Study in Public Schools

Stephen Prothero, as told to Patton Dodd

In the following viewpoint, Stephen Prothero, interviewed by Patton Dodd, contends that the Bible should be taught in public schools because Western and American civilizations are based on it. He argues that religion inspires people so it is important to be able to understand those beliefs, regardless of whether they originate with Christianity or Islam. Prothero is the chair of the Religion Department at Boston University and is the author of Religious Literacy: What Americans Need to Know.

As you read, consider the following questions:

1. According to Stephen Prothero, how did the events of September 11, 2001, change the way people feel about religion being taught in public schools?

Stephen Prothero, as told to Patton Dodd, "Should the Bible Be Taught in Public Schools? (Interview with Stephen Prothero)," Beliefnet.com, July 2007. Copyright © 2008 Beliefnet, Inc. Reproduced by permission.

2. In Prothero's opinion, why is it possible for the Bible to be taught objectively in public schools?

3. Why is the U.S. Supreme Court not to blame for religion not being taught in public schools, according to Prothero?

Patton Dodd: *You claim that Americans don't know much about religion, a fact that is well established by surveys testing religious knowledge. But why does it matter that Americans know the Five Pillars of Islam or basic facts about the Bible?*

Stephen Prothero: In a democracy, citizens are supposed to be involved. And we can't be involved on religiously inflected questions unless we know something about religion. On the home front, it's important to know something about Christianity and the Bible in order to hold politicians accountable. Especially in recent years, both Democrats and Republicans are appealing to religious reasons when they make arguments about abortion or stem cell research or the environment. And [for foreign policy], it's important to know something about Islam and other religions because religions motivate people— make them act for or against American interests.

You're calling on high schools and colleges to dramatically change their approach to teaching religion, which would require a major effort in terms of preparing curriculum, training educators, etc. How likely is it that we will see shifts in the ways that we teach religion in our schools?

Why do people always ask me how likely it is?

Maybe because that's the reflex thought to hearing someone say religion ought to be taught more in public schools. Given federalized testing, teacher shortages, etc., isn't it reasonable to ask how likely this is to happen?

Yeah, the reflex thought is it's unlikely. But it's not unlikely. That's my answer: It's not unlikely. There are a number of reasons. I'll do a few.

Okay.

Religion Plays an Important Role in Society

Most Americans are in favor of this. There has been some polling where people are asked, "How would you feel about having your children take courses about religion in the public schools?" And overwhelmingly people say yes, they're in favor of it. So, that's one thing.

Another is [that] since 9/11 [2001, terrorist attacks on America] things have really shifted on this question about religion. If you were a head-in-the-sand secularist back on September 10, 2001, you could get by because you could imagine that religion was going away in the world just like it had gone away in your life. After 9/11, you can't do that any more. People who do that seem really stupid. It's undeniable that religion is powerful and it's undeniable that it's something that we, for perfectly pragmatic political reasons, need to know something about.

Another reason is that the culture wars have really exaggerated how much contention there is about religion in the United States. There's a sense that public voices for religion are either right-wing fundamentalists or left-wing atheists. But that is a teeny, teeny portion of the American religious pie. The overwhelming majority of us are in the middle. And those people in the middle find this kind of proposal really reasonable and practical and sane.

The Bible Is the Basis for Western and American Civilizations

Your proposal is that schools dedicate a year to teaching religion—a semester to the Bible and a semester to the rest of world religions. Why do you advocate for schools to teach the Bible more than other religious subjects?

Because the Bible is the scripture of American politics. Because in American politics, the Judeo-Christian tradition is the tradition on which politicians make arguments. If you know a lot about Zoroastrianism, that doesn't help you to understand American politics and participate in it.

The question isn't what religion is true or most valuable. The question is, What religious traditions do you need to know something about in order to be an effective citizen? If you look at the congressional record, you're not going to see a lot of references to the Buddha and to the Bhagavad-Gita. But you're going to see tons of references to the Bible, to Armageddon, to apocalypse, to the Promised Land, to the Good Samaritan.

Similarly, if you stroll through your local museum and look at art, or if you read through the reading list of American literature for your local high school, you're going to find repeated references to the Bible. And if you don't understand those references you're going to be confused.

Whether you like it or not, whether you're an atheist or a Christian, whether you're a Jew or a Muslim, the fact of the matter is, the Bible is the text that in Western and American civilization has been most influential and, therefore, it's the text we need to know more about than we have to know about other texts.

Teaching About Religion Is Not the Same as Preaching About It

Perhaps the reason this is such a contentious issue is the problem of motive. How can we be certain of the motives of teachers who—

I thought you were going to ask about my motive. Because people do ask me about that.

I bet.

I've gotten so many e-mails from people saying, "You have a secret agenda. This is the back-door way of reintroducing Christianity and Christian teaching back into the public schools."

What do you say to that?

The Bible Is the Source for Common Ground

The Bible and Bible-centered Protestantism are central to U.S. history—to your history if you are American, whether you are Protestant or not. The founders had varied beliefs, writes the philosopher-historian Michael Novak in *On Two Wings*, but they found common ground "by appealing to the God of the Hebrews and the religious heritage of the Torah, a 'Biblical metaphysics.'"

David Gelernter,
"Why the Bible Belongs in America's Public Schools,"
Los Angeles Times, *May 27, 2005.*

That there are two ways of talking about religion. One is this devotional way where you talk about "my" religion and the question is about truth. And another is more objective and academic and frankly secular, where you can talk about religions as something that human beings do rather than something that's true.

So I think it's really important for people to understand that distinction between preaching religion and teaching about religion.

Absolutely agreed. Still, what haunts people when they think of the Bible being taught in public schools is that teachers cannot be trusted to be objective.

The way it's always asked me is, "Can we trust the committed Christians to do this?" But I always ask, "What about the committed atheists?"

But here's my answer: We do this all the time with other subjects. If somebody's a really conservative Republican or a really liberal Democrat and they're teaching political science in high school, we don't think that that's disqualifying. We just expect them to be careful. We expect them to check their biases. And that happens all the time.

If there's somebody in a literature class who hates poetry but loves novels, they have to teach poetry and they have to try to teach it as best as they can without telling the students all the time that they hate poetry.

Isn't there a big difference between loving Jesus and loving novels?

I just don't see it. I think [religion] is more dear to us. But in terms of the problem of bias, it's really the same. And every single day, in every single public school, we trust our public school teachers to be able to table, to some extent, the biases that they have. If they can't, we fire them. I don't see why we can't do this with religion.

I have colleagues who are born-again Christians. I have colleagues who are atheists. I have colleagues who are Muslims. And they do a responsible job teaching their subjects without trying to proselytize. I don't see why high school teachers can't do the same thing.

The reality is that we already have these courses. About one out of every twelve public school districts are teaching courses on the Bible. And presumably, those courses are being done pretty well. It's not like this as a novel idea. It's not like you have to create curricula out of nothing or teach training concepts out of nothing. This is already happening.

The Supreme Court Ruled That Teaching About Religion Is Constitutional

And yet, here you are writing a book based on the fact that Americans don't know enough about religion. Why is that? Why don't Americans know much about religion?

The first thing to say is that it's not the fault of the Supreme Court. The common wisdom is that a bunch of secular liberals on the Supreme Court pushed religion out of public schools when they banned prayer and devotional Bible reading in 1962 and 1963. And that's just not true. In those court cases and in the court cases that came before and after, the Supreme Court repeatedly said that although preaching religion is wrong, teaching about religion is constitutional. And not only is it constitutional, it's desirable.

You really can't be said to be educated, says the Supreme Court, if you don't know something about the Bible, Christianity and other world religions. They've said this in their rulings. You can go read them online.

So religious ignorance is not a recent development. You make the surprising argument that American religious history is partly to blame for the decline of religious knowledge in this country.

The historical argument that I make is that when Puritan culture was the dominant religious culture in the United States, in the Colonial and Early National periods, Protestant literacy went hand-in-hand with basic literacy. Part of being religious was being educated. That starts to go away in the middle of the 19th century with the rise of Evangelicalisms. As Puritanism yields to Evangelicalism, religious literacy starts to plummet.

Religious Knowledge Has Declined

Evangelicals emphasize reading the Bible and Bible knowledge. Why would Evangelicalism contribute to the decline of religious knowledge?

There are a lot of factors involved that I outline in the book. One is that that experience becomes more important than education. It becomes more important to love and have a relationship with Jesus than to know what Jesus had to say. You can see the shift in Sunday school materials, in sermons, in tracts. You also see it in the public schools where there are battles over what kind of Bibles to read. The Catholics want the Catholic Bibles and the Protestants want the King James and they can't agree, and so in many places in the middle of the 19th century, they finally just agree to get rid of the Bible [in public schools].

Then, as the Protestant denominations start to cooperate on a lot of social reform issues over the course of the 19th century on temperance, abolitionism, and women's rights, it becomes less and less important to know about the specific doctrines and teachings of your denomination. In fact, it becomes a barrier to cross-denominational cooperation. And so, people gradually start to forget what it is to be a Lutheran or a Methodist, a Baptist. And gradually, the doctrinal and the narrative elements of religion, which for me, sort of form the core of religious literacy, start to fade away as we emphasize other elements in religion, particularly the experiential and the moral.

It's fascinating and ironic that, as you argue, the failure of religious knowledge can be blamed on the most religiously fervent people in America. Among historians, is this the common explanation for the decline in religious literacy?

No. Pieces of it, but I like to think it's my own. I am a historian and so, to me, the most interesting parts of the book are the chapters where I argue that the demise of religious literacy came at the hands not of secular people, but religious people.

You place part of the blame on the great religious revivals in this country, the First and Second Great Awakenings.

Right, because they changed the way we do religion. The revivals tell us that religion is about feeling instead of about knowing. We rely on those revivals on unlettered preachers and we come to affirm a kind of romance where the less you know about religion, the more heartfelt you could be. Your religion is somehow more powerful and more imitable if it's not sullied by any knowledge—even, ironically, knowledge about the Bible.

> "*Rather than abandon public schools, leaders of this group [the religious right] see public schools—and the captive audiences therein—as plump targets for evangelism.*"

There Should Not Be Prayer and Bible Study in Public Schools

Rob Boston

In the following viewpoint, Rob Boston maintains that it is inappropriate for public school students to be taught about creationism and other beliefs of the religious right. Not only does Boston maintain that it is unconstitutional, but, he asserts, children are made to feel isolated if their personal religious beliefs are belittled. He argues that a teacher's job is to educate her students, not to convert them. Rob Boston is the assistant director of communications for Americans United for Separation of Church and State, an organization devoted to protecting religious liberty in the United States.

Rob Boston, "Putting an End to 'Teacher-Preachers' in Public Schools," *The Humanist*, vol. 67, May–June 2007, p. 38. Reproduced by permission of the author.

As you read, consider the following questions:

1. In Rob Boston's opinion, how did the actions taken by officials at Matthew LaClair's school punish LaClair and not his teacher, David Paszkiewicz?
2. According to the author, what percentage of children in the United State attend public schools?
3. What is "stealth evangelism," according to Boston?

Recently, a public high school teacher stood before his class and told the students that if they didn't accept Jesus Christ as their personal savior, they would go to hell. Furthermore, he added that evolution is a crock, and dinosaurs lived on Noah's ark.

Your first thought might be, where did this happen—Mississippi or rural Texas?

Try New Jersey—ten miles outside of New York City.

Matthew LaClair, a junior at Kearny High School in Kearny, New Jersey, grew frustrated when David Paszkiewicz, instructor of an honors history course, began veering off topic and delivering sermons. But LaClair didn't want to complain to school officials before he had proof, so he secretly taped Paszkiewicz's preaching.

"If you reject his gift of salvation, then you know where you belong," Paszkiewicz is heard saying on the tape. "He did everything in his power to make sure that you could go to heaven, so much so that he took your sins on his own body, suffered your pains for you, and he's saying, 'Please, accept me, believe.' If you reject that, you belong in hell."

Confronted with the tape, Paszkiewicz wasn't able to deny that he was preaching. He's now claiming he was set up by LaClair. If Paszkiewicz is to be believed, LaClair somehow tricked him into proselytizing as part of a plot to get the teacher in trouble: He has yet to explain exactly how or why LaClair might have done this.

Students Should Not Be Subjected to Preaching

Kearny school officials reacted to the flap in a most curious way. They claimed they would rein in Paszkiewicz, but to date most of their punitive actions have been directed at LaClair. The school system implemented a new policy barring students from secretly taping lectures, and they dispersed that particular history class, sending LaClair and his classmates off to other teachers.

The decision to break up the class has made LaClair less than popular. Apparently Paszkiewicz is a well-liked teacher, and some students are mad about being forced out of his class. Others accept Paszkiewicz's rather implausible version of events. LaClair has been ostracized, taunted, and even received a death threat.

LaClair's parents are insisting that the school protect their son; they are also considering legal action. At a recent meeting of the school board, LaClair said, "During the whole time I've been harassed and bullied, you've done nothing to defend me; you make it look like I've done something wrong."

The sad incident is a reminder that the religious neutrality of the U.S. public school system is never truly secure. It's remarkable and quite sad that incidents like this still occur forty-five years after the U.S. Supreme Court banned mandatory, school-sponsored devotional exercises.

The threats of hellfire were bad enough and the promotion of creationism only made things worse.

What's worse is that the Kearny flap isn't an isolated example. Every year attorneys at Americans United for Separation of Church and State receive dozens of complaints about inappropriate forms of religion in public schools. Examples range from school-sponsored prayer at mandatory assemblies and in-school Bible distribution by Gideons to efforts to teach creationism and adopt Bible classes that reflect fundamentalist dogma.

Using Public Schools to Preach About the Bible

For many years religious right leaders have talked openly about abandoning the secular public school system, which they believe to be damned. One ambitious group formed in 1997 called itself "Exodus 2000," hoping that all fundamentalist parents would remove their children from public schools within three years.

It didn't happen. Despite all the talk about the growth of private education and home schooling, the fact is that public education serves 90 percent of U.S. children. That number has remained constant for many years and it's a figure that excites other factions of the religious right. Rather than abandon public schools, leaders of this group see public schools—and the captive audiences therein—as plump targets for evangelism.

This "stealth evangelism" takes many forms. Americans United regularly receives complaints about groups offering free assemblies to public schools. The event usually either turns into a sermon or students are pressured to attend a "party" later that evening that is really a revival service at a local church. (A tip for school officials: be wary of free assemblies, especially when the group offering them has the word "ministry" appended to its name. Even if an organization disguises its true intent, a few minutes of research on the Web can usually smoke out the proselytizers.)

Preaching teachers are more problematic because sometimes they fly under the radar, offering in-class sermons without the sanction or knowledge of school officials. Many young people look at teachers as authority figures and are reluctant to challenge them in class. Others fear the type of ostracism and harassment that LaClair is undergoing.

In Paszkiewicz's case, his stunt was doubly offensive. The threats of hellfire were bad enough and the promotion of creationism only made things worse. One can only wonder what

Public Schools Must Remain Religiously Neutral

Misguided individuals and powerful sectarian lobbies in Washington continue to press for religious majority rule in the nation's public schools. They advocate for school prayer amendments and other measures that would permit government-sponsored worship in the schools. They want their beliefs taught in the public schools and hope to use the public schools as instruments of evangelism.

Americans must resist these efforts. They must protect the religious neutrality of public education. Being neutral on religion is not the same as being hostile toward it. In a multi-faith, religiously diverse society such as ours, neutrality is the appropriate stance for the government to take toward religion. Under this principle, public schools can allow for individual student religious expression without endorsing or promoting any specific faith.

Americans United for Separation of Church and State,
Prayer and the Public Schools:
Religion, Education and Your Rights,
2007. www.au.org.

the school's science faculty thinks about a history teacher's decision to push pseudo-science in class. And how long would Paszkiewicz have gotten away with any of this had he been a Muslim, a humanist, or even a Jehovah's Witness?

Public Education Is Not a Tool for Indoctrination

Legitimate instruction about religion as an academic subject in public schools isn't a problem. As long as it's done in a non-dogmatic manner intended to educate, not indoctrinate, such instruction can be a valuable addition to the curriculum.

The introduction of sectarian dogma is something else entirely. Not only is it unconstitutional, it's just plain rude. What Paszkiewicz essentially told all of the Jews, atheists, Buddhists, and mainline Christians in his class was: The religion or moral philosophy your parents chose to raise you with is wrong; I know better than they do, and you should discard your family's religion in favor of my alternative.

So much for parental rights.

Public education officials in Kearny have some work to do. First, they need to apologize to LaClair and his family and make sure the harassment stops. Then they need to rein in Paszkiewicz.

All of us have a job too. The separation of church and state will never be fully respected in public schools if we aren't vigilant. We must never assume that this issue is settled. The law has been on our side for nearly fifty years, yet we still find ourselves fighting attempts to inject sectarianism into our public schools.

One of the most important things we can do is support those who are willing to stick their necks out in defense of liberty. Disputes over religion in public schools bring out the worst in some people. Ironically, it is often the "holier-than-thou" brigade that is the first to weigh in with verbal abuse, threats, and intimidation.

If the people who oppose the religious right's attempt to "Christianize" our public schools feel isolated and scorned, they might take a pass the next time a violation occurs. We need to work to create an atmosphere where whistleblowers like Matthew LaClair are treated like heroes, not villains, for speaking out for their constitutional rights.

"*Government shall not favor religion over 'no religion.' RFRA [Religious Freedom Restoration Act] legally endorses discrimination against those who do not endorse organized religion.*"

Religious Freedom Laws Are Discriminatory and Unnecessary

Institute for Humanist Studies

In the following viewpoint, the Institute for Humanist Studies (IHS) argues against a Religious Freedom Restoration Act (RFRA) in New York State. The group maintains that the law is unnecessary because past court cases in the state were decided in favor of religious freedom. It also contends that such a law puts the government in the position of becoming involved in and promoting religion. The institute asserts that such laws give special rights to religious people that are not extended to all. The IHS is a group dedicated to publicizing humanism to increase public consciousness and knowledge.

Institute for Humanist Studies, "Why Does the IHS Oppose RFRA in New York State?" 2007. Reproduced by permission.

As you read, consider the following questions:

1. In the opinion of IHS, in what ways would some organized religions be given "special privileges" if the RFRA is passed in New York State?

2. According to the IHS, how would the RFRA be a threat to secularism?

3. How many nonreligious New Yorkers were there in 2001, and how many Americans declared "no religion" in the same year?

As U.S. Supreme Court Justice Antonin Scalia said, "Who can possibly be against the abstract proposition that government should not, even in its general, nondiscriminatory laws, place unreasonable burdens upon religious practices? Unfortunately, however, that abstract proposition must ultimately be reduced to concrete cases." In those concrete cases it is evident that not only is RFRA [Religious Freedom Restoration Act] unnecessary, but unjust.

What RFRA theoretically promises differs greatly from its practical application. In practice, RFRA is redundant and discriminatory. The application of RFRA will call into question many secular laws that have nothing to do with religion and exist to protect all New Yorkers regardless of religion or creed.

RFRA is unnecessary because it is redundant on both the federal level and state level. Our right to religious freedom is already protected in the U.S. Bill of Rights:

> Congress shall make no law respecting an establishment of religion, or prohibiting the free exercise thereof . . .
> —*First Amendment to the U.S. Constitution*

Additionally, the New York State Constitution also clearly guarantees free religious exercise:

> The free exercise and enjoyment of religious profession and worship, without discrimination or preference, shall forever

be allowed in this state to all humankind; and no person shall be rendered incompetent to be a witness on account of his or her opinions on matters of religious belief; but the liberty of conscience hereby secured shall not be so construed as to excuse acts of licentiousness, or justify practices inconsistent with the peace or safety of this state. (Amended by vote of the people November 7, 2001.)

—Article I, section 3, Bill of Rights,
the Constitution of the State of New York

Religious Freedom Is Already Protected Under the Law

RFRA advocates want you to believe that your right to religious freedom is insecure. But on what grounds do they make this claim? So far New York State has dealt fairly with cases of religious freedom. The system is working. Religious freedom is not in danger in New York State. In case after case where New Yorkers claimed their religious freedom was infringed upon, the courts ruled in their favor.

For example, Gov. [Eliot] Spitzer endorses RFRA legislation. But even his June 11 [2007] press release in support of RFRA states (emphasis added):

> As Attorney General, Spitzer brought numerous cases defending workers' rights to observe certain religious customs and practices. One such case involved a Jewish repairman who was required to work on the Sabbath. Another case involved a deliveryman who was ordered to cut the dreadlocks customary to his religion. Still another case involved a female medical student who was required to wear clothing considered immodest in her religion. *In each of these cases, the courts ruled that the religious observances were not disruptive to employers and should be accommodated.* The new legislation would ensure that such reasonable accommodation of religious customs becomes a standard principle of New York law.

RFRA Would Give Special Preference to Certain Religions

The motivations behind passing RFRA in New York State appear murky and seem to have less to do with religious freedom than special privileges. One possible motivation behind RFRA is to give certain organized religions access to goods, resources, and services that are not available to the average citizen. For instance, RFRA could potentially make it easier for Catholic priests [to] deal with accusations of child molestation internally. It could allow particular sects to use drugs that are outlawed for the rest of the population. It could allow churches and temples to ignore zoning requirements that apply to everyone else—endangering the health and safety of New Yorkers and our built and natural environment. RFRA's far reaching scope could affect child abuse issues, anti-discrimination laws, polygamy, animal rights, parking, housing, zoning, drug use, and so much more.

RFRA essentially establishes special rights for religious believers that are not available to other Americans. In this way, it is discriminatory and unfair. Government is not supposed to interfere with religious practices or give preference to any specific religion over other religions. Government shall not favor religion over "no religion." RFRA legally endorses discrimination against those who do not endorse organized religion. In 2001, there were 1.9 million nonreligious New Yorkers, nearly double the figure from 10 years ago. (More than 29 million Americans reported "no religion" in 2001.)

RFRA is problematic in that it not only pits religious against non-religious, but religion against religion. Those organized religions that have wide appeal or have already been embraced by the mainstream are likely to be seen as having a more justified claim to protecting their religious practices than those religions that are seen as taboo, controversial, and less popular. As U.S. Supreme Court Justice John Paul Stevens

Religion Does Not Give Permission to Take Advantage of the Law

As a core principle of the First Amendment, the freedom of ideas is absolute, but the freedom to act on those ideas is not. The government has the mandate to ensure that actions (whether based on religion or not) do not endanger our society or specific individual members of our society. For example, the Christian Identity Movement is founded on white supremacist theology and because of the First Amendment its ideas are not illegal; however, it is common sense that if its racist theology produces actions that incite or cause harm, these actions cannot be exempted under the claim of religious freedom.

Regrettably, RFRA [Religious Freedom Restoration Act] blurs this line between ideas and actions and gives the members of religious groups the license to defy any law if they believe it infringes on their religious freedom. As Tim Gordinier, a professor at [State University of New York] SUNY–Potsdam, and former director of Public Policy and Education at the Institute for Humanist Studies, explains, "The Free Exercise Clause only meant that you couldn't single out religious people for discriminatory treatment—not that they had the special privilege to ignore laws the rest of us are bound to obey." RFRA allows members of religious groups to violate the law based on their theological beliefs; however, violation of the law for some other worthy, yet nonreligious, moral, political, philosophical, medical, or artistic reason does not get the same consideration.

Secular Coalition for America,
"Religious Freedom Restoration Act (RFRA);
Religious Land Use and Institutionalized Persons Act (RLUIPA),"
2007. www.secular.org.

pointed out, RFRA is a "law respecting an establishment of religion" that violates the First Amendment to the Constitution—not protects it.

Educating the Public About Existing Religious Protections Is More Important

The Institute for Humanist Studies opposes all proposed RFRA legislation. At best RFRA is redundant, and at worst it endangers centuries of secular legislation. Gov. Spitzer's proposed . . . legislation is ill defined and therefore especially dangerous in its potential for unintended consequences.

While Assembly Speaker Sheldon Silver's . . . bill attempts to be less vague than Spitzer, Silver's proposal is still at best redundant and at worst harmful. The more that legislators like Silver work to draft less harmful versions of RFRA, the more obvious it becomes that RFRA is not needed in the first place.

Instead of drafting new legislation, the Institute for Humanist Studies feels that the state government should do more to educate the public about existing protections for and limitations of the free exercise of religion.

RFRA Could Reverse Far-Reaching Decisions

RFRA is an attempt to circumvent the U.S. Supreme Court's 1990 *Employment Division v. Smith* on religious freedom. By looking at cases where the courts used the "*Smith* ruling" we can see where decisions might be different if RFRA were enacted.

Do you think the following court rulings should be reversed? RFRA could reverse these decisions:

- A church in New Mexico claimed that a licensing requirement for a child care center (i.e., rule prohibiting spanking) violated their free exercise rights. The court denied the claim under *Smith* [*Health Services Division v. Temple Baptist Church* (1991)].

- A Catholic hospital in Pennsylvania sought to preclude application of the Federal Age Discrimination in Employment Act. The court rejected the hospital's free exercise argument citing Smith [*Lukaszewski v. Nazareth Hospital* (1991)].

- A married male paramedic sued alleging that his employer's requiring him to stay overnight with a female paramedic at a station while on duty conflicted with his religious beliefs. The court rejected his free exercise claim, citing Smith [*Miller v. Drennon* (1992)].

- The state medical examiner in Michigan ordered an autopsy performed on the plaintiff's son after he was killed in an automobile accident. The plaintiff, who was Jewish, alleged that performance of the autopsy violated her free exercise rights. The court denied her claim, relying on Smith [*Montgomery v. County of Clinton* (1990)].

- A wrongful death case was filed on behalf of a Jehovah's Witness who was hit by a car and injured. The Jehovah's Witness later died after allegedly refusing a blood transfusion on religious grounds. The plaintiff argued that failure to mitigate damages for wrongful death is a violation of the plaintiff's free exercise rights. (In other words, if Person A inflicts a non life-threatening injury upon a Jehovah's Witness and that Jehovah's Witness refuses medical treatment on religious grounds and later dies from that refusal of medical care, Person A is responsible for the death of the Jehovah's Witness.) The court rejected this argument, relying in part on Smith [*Munn v. Algee* (1991)].

- A Michigan court ruled that the state's requirement that nonpublic schools use state certified teachers did not violate the defendant's free exercise rights, applying the *Smith* test [*People v. DeJonge* (1991)].

- An FBI agent refused for religious reasons to be involved in a domestic security and terrorism investigation. The court denied the claim based upon *Smith* [*Ryan v. United States* (1991)].

- A Church in New York opposed application of landmarking ordinances to buildings owned by the church. The court rejected the church's free exercise argument based upon *Smith* [*St. Bartholomew's Church v. City of New York and Landmarks Preservation Commission* (1990)].

- An Illinois plaintiff argued that the Boy Scouts violated Title II in denying him admission because he refused to take the "Duty to God" oath. The Scouts argued that to require them to admit those who denied a belief in God violated their free exercise rights. Relying on *Smith*, the court rejected the Scouts' argument [*Welsh v. Boy Scouts of America*, 1990].

Although [Governor Spitzer's proposed legislation] could reverse all of the cases above, it is not clear if [Assembly Speaker Silver's] would reverse [*Lukaszewski* or *Welsh*]. While [Silver's] prohibits discrimination, it is not clear that this law would protect atheists from religious discrimination. Discrimination against atheists is still widely acceptable by mainstream America.

> *"Given the centrality of freedom of speech and religion to the American concept of personal liberty, it is altogether reasonable to conclude that both should be treated with the highest degree of respect."*

Religious Freedom Laws Are Necessary

Christopher J. Klicka

In the following viewpoint, Christopher J. Klicka argues that secularism threatens to overpower religious liberty. He cites the U.S. Supreme Court decision in City of Boerne v. Flores, *in 1997, which declared the Religious Freedom Restoration Act to be unconstitutional. Klicka contends that each state should pass its own Religious Freedom Act to ensure that parents can freely practice their religion, particularly for those parents who home-school their children. Klicka is senior counsel of the Home School Legal Defense Association, and is the author of* The Right Choice: Home Schooling *and* The Heart of Home Schooling.

Christopher J. Klicka, "Religious Freedom Is Endangered: How We Can Fight Back," *Practical Homeschooling*, vol. 67, November-December 2005, p. 16. Copyright ©1993–2008 Home Life, Inc. Reproduced by permission.

As you read, consider the following questions:

1. According to Christopher Klicka, what did the Supreme Court decide in *City of Boerne v. Flores*?

2. In the author's opinion, how does a state Religious Freedom Act protect the religious rights of homeschooled children?

3. According to the majority of justices in *City of Boerne v. Flores*, what did the right to practice one's religious beliefs have to be combined with in order to be given more than a reasonableness test?

On June 25, 1997, the U.S. Supreme Court, by a 6-3 majority, ruled the Religious Freedom Restoration Act (RFRA) unconstitutional in *City of Boerne v. Flores*. This was a devastating blow to our religious freedom in this country.

The facts of the case are this: After the city of Boerne denied a building permit to a church because the church building was located in a historic district, Catholic Archbishop Flores of San Antonio appealed this decision, arguing that this denial of the church's right to expand to accommodate its growing congregation violated the church's right to freely exercise its religious beliefs as protected by the RFRA. The U.S. Supreme Court ruled against the church and in the process struck down the RFRA, which was the highest level of protection of our religious liberty available.

Since this extremely harmful U.S. Supreme Court *Boerne* decision, state and federal courts have diminished religious freedom in many ways. For example:

- The long-standing practice of pastor-laity confidentiality has been repeatedly violated

- A Catholic hospital was denied state accreditation for refusing to teach abortion techniques

- There have been conflicts with zoning ordinances, such as shutting down a church ministry to the homeless because it was located on the second floor of a building with no elevator

- A church was prohibited by a local city ordinance from feeding more than 50 poor people per day

The list goes on and on. This subtle erosion of our religious liberty by the courts who are applying the *Boerne* ruling is gradually removing one of the bedrock defenses of homeschooling.

But there is hope.

Each State Must Have Its Own Religious Freedom Act

Several years ago, HSLDA [Home School Legal Defense Association] and a broad coalition of organizations worked very hard to get the federal RFRA enacted. Since it was struck down, other attempts at the federal level to resolve the religious freedom crisis have been misguided or have failed.

HSLDA, therefore, along with several other pro-religious freedom organizations and many state homeschool organizations, is urging all of the 50 states to pass their own Religious Freedom Act [RFA] to counter the *Boerne* case's devastating impact on religious freedom.

As of August 2005, by God's grace, more than a quarter of the states have acted to protect the religious freedom of the citizens in their states. Rhode Island, Connecticut, Florida, Illinois, Arizona, South Carolina, Texas, Idaho, New Mexico, Missouri, Pennsylvania, and Oklahoma have passed their own state Religious Freedom Acts. Alabama made religious freedom even more secure by specifically amending their state constitution to recognize religious freedom as a fundamental right protected by the compelling interest test.

HSLDA's legal staff has worked with religious freedom coalitions in the states (and the national state religious freedom coalition), helped draft legislation, lobbied individual state legislators, attorney generals, and governor offices, sent out numerous alerts, and provided testimony at some legislative hearings in order to advance these Religious Freedom Acts. The phone calls of thousands of homeschoolers particularly contributed to the passage of the RFRAs in Illinois, Arizona, Texas, South Carolina, Idaho, New Mexico, and Oklahoma. The Illinois act was successful after two HSLDA alerts and tremendous outpouring of calls by homeschoolers convinced legislators to override the governor's veto.

HSLDA and homeschoolers have brought significant pressure on the state legislatures of Virginia and Oregon along with much work in Louisiana, California, and Hawaii, but the fruits of their labors have not yet been realized. In 1999, Religious Freedom Restoration Acts were passed by both houses in New Mexico and California, only to have them vetoed by the governors. However, in April 2000, HSLDA and homeschoolers were able to convince both the New Mexico legislature and Governor Gary Johnson to re-pass and authorize a RFRA bill. Also encouraging is the fact that RFRA bills have continued to be introduced in numerous states during the 2004 and 2005 legislative sessions, although not all have passed.

RFAs Protect the Rights of the Homeschooled

We have used these state Religious Freedom Acts to help homeschoolers escape onerous homeschool requirements. For example, homeschoolers who have religious reasons for homeschooling have invoked the Florida Religious Freedom Act that HSLDA helped pass a few years ago. This act provides religious homeschoolers with a legal means to say "no" to the portfolio review of all their school records as allowed by Florida law. For some homeschool families the portfolio review by the local school district is offensive to their religious beliefs. By invoking the Religious Freedom Act these home-schoolers have forced the state to prove that the fulfillment of a portfolio review "furthers a compelling state interest" and is the "least restrictive means" of fulfilling its interest that children be educated. Instead of going to court, school districts have just exempted homeschoolers from invasive portfolio reviews!

In Pennsylvania, we are using that state's Religious Freedom Act to successfully fight against a very cumbersome and regulatory homeschool law that has substantially burdened families for years. We currently have about 50 families who are no longer following these onerous restrictions after invoking the RFA and are being left alone. We have a half dozen more families that we helped in court to win their religious exemption under the Act.

All freedom-loving homeschoolers should be prepared to call their legislators to support their state's Religious Freedom Act in order to save religious freedom. . . . Don't let one decision by the U.S. Supreme Court denigrate this priceless inalienable right!

Congress Should Interpret the Constitution, Not the Supreme Court

The RFRA was originally drafted in response to a 1990 U.S. Supreme Court decision (*Smith II*) in which the Court gave the lowest level of protection to religious liberty—one of the foundational freedoms of homeschooling. Using this ruling, a state could override an individual's right to freely exercise his religious beliefs merely by proving that its regulation was "reasonable."

HSLDA helped form the coalition which drafted and promoted the RFRA. Three years later, Congress passed the RFRA and President Bill Clinton signed it into law, reversing the disastrous effects of *Smith II* by restoring religious freedom as a fundamental right.

Religious Freedom
Is a Fundamental Right

[In response to a question about the greatest threat to religious liberty in the United States, Kevin Seamus Hasson stated:] The biggest threat comes from people who think that religious truth is the enemy of human freedom—that the only good religion is a relativist one [truth and moral values are relative to the people holding them and are not absolute]. When [writer] Andrew Sullivan says something called "fundamentalism" is the seedbed of terrorism, he's making this fundamental mistake. At a more amusing level, when school officials ban Valentine's cards (because after all, the holiday is named after St. Valentine), but tell schoolchildren they can still send each other "special person cards," that's the same basic error. In Lansing, Michigan, public school bureaucrats worried that the Easter Bunny isn't secular enough, now offer "Breakfast with the Special Bunny."

Practically speaking, the threat comes from lawyers, judges, and political elites who think that nativity scenes and menorahs are like secondhand smoke—something that decent people shouldn't be exposed to in the public square.

This theory of our Constitution is not only wrong, it is inhuman. If we frame the battle for religious liberty correctly, both the courts and the vast majority of Americans—and not just Christian conservatives—will be on our side.

Kevin Seamus Hasson, as told to National Review Online,
"Fighting for the Right to Be Wrong,"
October 18, 2005. www.nationalreview.com.

The RFRA affirmed a 1963 decision (*Sherbert v. Verner*) in which the U.S. Supreme Court held that in order for a state's regulation to prevail over an individual's right to freely exercise his religious belief, the state had to prove that its regulation was "essential" to achieve a compelling interest. In addition, the state had to provide evidence that it was using the "least restrictive means" to accomplish this compelling interest. Under this high standard of review, the free exercise of religion was usually upheld over restrictive state regulations.

However, in the City of Boerne case, the U.S. Supreme Court held that the power of Congress under Section 5 of the Fourteenth Amendment is limited to "enforcing the provisions of the Fourteenth Amendment." In the Court's opinion, Congress does not have the authority to determine what constitutes a constitutional violation. The Court held that the RFRA went too far in attempting to change the substantive law of constitutional protections. According to the *Boerne* decision, Congress can make determinations as to the proper interpretation of the Constitution, but courts ultimately have the authority to determine if Congress has exceeded its own constitutional bounds. In other words, the U.S. Supreme Court, not Congress, is the final arbiter in interpreting the Constitution.

Unfortunately, our conservative friends—the late Justice [William] Rehnquist and Justices [Antonin] Scalia and [Clarence] Thomas—joined with the majority in knocking our First Amendment right down from its lofty fundamental right status to a simple garden variety category. The Court ruled that only when a person's claim to freely exercise a religious belief is combined with another fundamental right still receiving the protection of the compelling interest test (in a "hybrid situation"), such as freedom of speech, freedom of the press, or the fundamental right of parents to direct the education and upbringing of their children, will it be given more than a simple reasonableness test.

Smith Decision Ignores the Intent of the Founding Fathers

Dissenting in the minority with Justices [Stephen] Breyer and [David] Souter, Justice [Sandra Day] O'Connor stated that the Court should have used this case to revisit the *Smith* decision of 1990 since *Smith* had so drastically redefined the standard of review of the Free Exercise Clause, departing from decades of Supreme Court precedent.

> [T]he Court's rejection of this principle in *Smith* is supported neither by precedent nor as discussed . . . by history. The decision has harmed religious liberty. The historical evidence casts doubt on the Court's current interpretation of the Free Exercise Clause.

O'Connor gave a stirring review of the importance of religious freedom in our country, quoting a number of state religious freedom charters. She noted that:

> [E]arly in our country's history, several colonies acknowledged that freedom to pursue one's chosen religious beliefs was an essential liberty. Moreover, these colonies appear to recognize that government should interfere in religious matters only when necessary to protect the civil peace or to prevent licentiousness.

She further explained that every state constitution included the right to freely exercise religious beliefs. She quoted James Madison and Thomas Jefferson in summary, explaining,

> "To Madison, then, duties to God were superior to duties to civil authorities—the ultimate loyalty was owed to God above all . . . the idea that civil obligations are subordinate to religious duty is consonant that government must accommodate, where possible, those religious practices that conflict with religious law."

O'Connor concluded,

"It has long been the Court's position that freedom of speech a right enumerated only a few words after the rights to Free Exercise has a special Constitutional status. Given the centrality of freedom of speech and religion to the American concept of personal liberty, it is altogether reasonable to conclude that both should be treated with the highest degree of respect. The rule the Court declared in *Smith* does not faithfully serve the purpose of the Constitution. Accordingly, I believe it essential for the Court to reconsider its holding in *Smith*."

Unfortunately, this dissent, although correct, was ignored.

Periodical Bibliography

The following articles have been selected to supplement the diverse views presented in this chapter.

Rob Boston — "The Bible Makes a Comeback in Public Schools," *The Humanist*, March-April 2006.

Paul Boudreau — "Hold Your Fire!" *U.S. Catholic*, December 2007.

Gary B. Christenot — "Why I'm Against Pre-Game Prayers: An Evangelical Christian's Story," *Church & State*, October 2006.

Tom Flynn — "Discrimination Against Christians? Oh, Please . . ." *Free Inquiry*, April-May 2005.

David Gelernter — "Lincoln's Words, Our Pledge," *Los Angeles Times*, November 18, 2005.

Michelle Goldbert — "The Rise of Christian Nationalism," *The Humanist*, September-October 2007.

Michael Jinkins — "Bible Classes in Public Schools," *Church & State*, May 2007.

Patrick Kucera — "A Cadet's Oath," *The Humanist*, September-October 2007.

Neal McCluskey — "Public Schooling's Divisive Effect," *USA Today*, September 2007.

Dennis Prager — "America Founded to Be Free, Not Secular," January 3, 2007. www.townhall.com.

William Raspberry — "Understanding Their Fears," *Washington Post*, June 21, 2004.

CHAPTER 4

What Is the Future of Atheism?

Chapter Preface

In 1859, Charles Darwin's theory of natural selection—*On the Origin of Species*—was published. In 2007, the Creation Museum, located in Petersburg, Kentucky, opened its doors to make the case against Darwinism.

Established by Answers in Genesis (AiG), a ministry devoted to defending Christianity and to showing how the book of Genesis provides answers to the universe's and man's beginnings, the museum asserts that everything in the universe can be explained by the Bible. The exhibits indicate that Earth was created in six days, the oldest fossils only date back 6,000 years, and humans and dinosaurs interacted. Writes Sarah Pride in an article for *Practical Homeschooling*, "First, a word on what you will not find at the Creation Museum. You will not find an esoteric, technical contrast of evolutionary and creationist scientific research. There's no need. The Answers in Genesis folks have always argued (and it's true!) that the difference between evolutionists and creationists is a matter of framework. Scientists take the same facts and fit them as best as they can into their framework of choice. The deciding point, then, is which framework best fits all the facts of life. In the museum, AiG asks the tough cultural questions for which evolution has no answers and shows how they fit alongside science into the Biblical creationist worldview."

Opponents argue that the museum incorrectly presents what is written in the Bible as fact. Critics of the Creation Museum contend that one can accept scientific facts about the beginnings of the universe and still believe in God. In an article for *The Cincinnati Post*, Lawrence M. Kraus maintains that "What [Answers in Genesis founder] Ken Ham and his colleagues are doing is not only an educational travesty of science, it is unfair to religion. Religion doesn't have to be bad science, and similarly bad science should not be defended simply because it might have a religious basis. And it is also unfair to children to convey the impression that unless one believes the earth was created in six days, one's faith is not consistent, and to accept the overwhelming scientific evidence of a 14-billion-year-old universe might be akin to eternal damnation."

Reconciling the views of atheists, who believe that science and reason can answer questions about the universe, with the religious, who accept the Bible as literal truth, is examined in this chapter. The authors of the viewpoints in this chapter also explore atheism's future, and whether atheism is—or should be—a religion.

> "We need to change people's minds with
> the same message of hope, peace, and
> love that religions offer. (They do offer
> it, even if they often fall short.)"

Atheism Has a Future

Gene Madeo

*In the following viewpoint, Gene Madeo contends that atheism
will have a future when nonbelievers begin to offer their vision
in a more constructive, positive manner. He contends that atheism is—and should be—a viable alternative to organized religion, and the politics of the religious right, but that its appeal is
being limited by negative attacks on the beliefs of the religious.
Madeo, who lives in Riverside, California, argues that atheists
need to formulate a plan to convince people that atheism offers
them more than religion does.*

As you read, consider the following questions:

1. According to Gene Madeo, why have Sam Harris and
   other atheists emerged as spokespeople for atheism?
2. What does Gene Madeo mean by "we may well end up
   winning some major battle, but end up losing the war"?

Gene Madeo, "The Future of Atheism and Agnosticism," *Humanist Network News*, August 1, 2007. Reproduced by permission.

3. In the author's opinion, what three steps should atheists and agnostics take to encourage more people to become nonbelievers?

As a non-believer, I have felt like a minority all of my adult life, and have often been afraid to openly express and share my beliefs and ideas. As minorities, it is easy for atheists and agnostics to express anger, frustration, and disappointment at how we are depicted and treated by believers and defend ourselves.

We have certainly been victims, and we always have been a small minority. The political religious right agenda in the U.S. for the last six years has been rather scary, demonstrating in real terms how religion and religious people can be dangerous. A direct result of it has been the emergence of Sam Harris and others, who are doing a fantastic job of pointing out the flaws and dangers of religious belief.

Should atheists and agnostics be angry fighters for legitimacy and dignity? If history is any guide, we should certainly never allow ourselves to be forced into a minority status. Sam Harris and some of our other spokespersons feel that indeed we are in danger and need to be fighting back—and hard.

Give People a Positive Reason to Become Atheist

They may be correct. For the first time in a long time, atheism and agnosticism are receiving a lot of attention, much of it positive, because the arguments are so powerful in today's world of religious activism and extremism. What I fear, however, is that today's momentum will hit an impassable wall of resistance because most people will still see atheists and agnostics as negative-oriented "spoilers" with nothing better to offer than what religion already does.

We may well end up winning some major battles, but end up losing the war (again), because we are not likely going to

Atheism Should Follow the Example of the Stem Cell Research Debate

One success story has come in the debate over human embryonic stem cells, a leading example of how scientists can effectively engage the public on controversial findings. In the weeks following Bush's 2001 compromise decision on stem cell research funding, more than 60 percent of the public supported the president's policy. But six years later, public opinion has shifted. In news coverage and campaigns, funding advocates have emphasized not the technical details of the research but the promise of new therapies and the resultant potential for economic growth.

Matthew C. Nisbet and Chris Mooney, "Thanks for the Facts. Now Sell Them," Washington Post, *April 15, 2007, p. B3.*

win this ideological war with criticism, argument, attack, and anger. Still, I give Sam Harris and others a lot of credit for forcing the issue with powerful arguments. But if powerful arguments were all that was needed, atheists and agnostics would not be the small minority they are today.

There have been powerful arguments in the past as well. Yes, we need scientists, theologians, philosophers, and other professionals to defend atheism and argue effectively in academic circles concerning the defects of religion. At the same time, most people are not receptive, but instead react negatively, to attacks against their beliefs.

I suggest that the only way atheists and agnostics will ever reach believers is by offering people a joyful, wonderful alternative to religion. To do so, we need to understand why religions are so successful. We are not doing this, and this is where our energy should be directed. We need to change people's minds with the same message of hope, peace, and love that religions offer. (They do offer it, even if they often fall short.)

We need to satisfy the same wants, needs, and desires that religion does. But if all we offer is criticism, argument, and anger, very few will listen to us. Unless atheists and agnostics somehow can satisfy the same needs, wants, and desires that are satisfied by religion, we will always be a very small minority.

When the believer asks, "what does the Atheistic and Agnostic life offer me and why is your way of life better?" we should have some great answers. We need to distance ourselves from the usual answer: "It's a more sensible, intelligent view of life, and a better way of life"—because it is not necessarily so.

Make Atheism a Viable Alternative to Religion

In my own quest over many years, I have been disappointed in what I've found as an alternative to religion, whether it was a group of atheists, humanists, secular humanists, freethinkers, or others. They always seemed angry, spending most of their time defending atheism, and criticizing religion and a belief in God.

Believers, in contrast, usually had pleasant dispositions and were involved in all kinds of enjoyable, and uplifting community activities. Adding to the contrast was the fact that you could drive around on any day and see tons of cars in church parking lots, yet you had a difficult time getting 30 atheists to attend a monthly meeting. Atheism may be right, but it was losing the battle with religion. "Why?" I asked myself.

My answer is that most non-believers 1) have failed to understand that religions satisfy very important needs, wants, and desires; 2) don't study and analyze how and why religions satisfy those needs, wants, and desires; and 3) do not work conscientiously to come up with a viable alternative that can satisfy most or all of those needs, wants, and desires that religion fulfills.

In general terms, my plan for the future of atheism is to

- Embark on local, national, and international campaigns to present people with a viable alternative to religion that focuses on love and reverence for all human beings.

- Leave the arguing to the theologians and scientists. In everyday life and in our campaign to elevate atheism to a higher position of respect in society, renounce all criticisms of religion and belief in God, and focus primarily on presenting a viable alternative to religion.

- Formulate a joyful, uplifting, passionate, and powerful message about atheism.

- Build a headquarters, and throughout the country and the world, support the movement with structures and purposes similar to churches.

- Satisfy the same needs, wants, and desires that religions do, even if in a different form.

> *"[Atheism's] uncompromising and de-*
> *finitive denial of God is now seen as*
> *arrogant and repressive, rather than as*
> *principled and moral."*

Atheism Does Not Have a Future

Alister McGrath

In the following viewpoint, Alister McGrath argues that atheism does not have a future because of its inability to offer people more than an intellectual argument that holds no emotional appeal. He also contends that its image has been tarnished by dictatorial regimes that claimed to be atheistic. McGrath maintains that there has been a resurgent interest in religion, especially Islam, because atheists seem unable to change their stated belief that God does not exist. Alister McGrath is a professor of history theology at Oxford University.

As you read, consider the following questions:

1. According to Alister McGrath, what means did Vladimir Lenin use to ensure that the Russian people accepted atheism?

Alister McGrath, "The Incoming Sea of Faith," *The Spectator*, September 18, 2004, p. 12.

2. What event of 1989 helped lead to atheism's association with oppressive force, according to the author?

3. In McGrath's opinion, which religion has become the most vocal and critical opponent of Christianity?

When I was an atheist back in the 1960s, its future seemed assured. I grew up in Northern Ireland, where religious tensions and violence had alienated many from Christianity. Like so many disaffected young people then, I rejected religion as oppressive, hypocritical, a barbarous relic of the past. The sociologists were predicting that religion would soon die out; if not, suitably enlightened governments and social agencies could ensure that it was relegated to the margins of culture, the last refuge of the intellectually feeble and socially devious. The sooner it was eliminated, the better place the world would be.

Atheism then had the power to command my mind and excite my heart. It made sense of things, and offered a powerful vision of the future. The world would be a better place once religion ended. It was simply a matter of time, judiciously aided by direct action here and there. Although I am no longer an atheist, I retain a profound respect for its aspirations for humanity and legitimate criticisms of dysfunctional religion. Yet the sun seems to be setting on this shopworn, jaded and tired belief system, which now lacks the vitality that once gave it passion and power.

To suggest that atheism is a belief system or faith will irritate some of its followers. For them, atheism is not a belief; it is the Truth. There is no god, and those who believe otherwise are deluded, foolish or liars (to borrow from the breezy rhetoric of Britain's favourite atheist, the scientific populariser turned atheist propagandist Richard Dawkins). But it's now clear that the atheist case against God has stalled. Surefire philosophical arguments against God have turned out to be circular and self-referential.

The most vigorous intellectual critique of religion now comes from Dawkins, who has established himself as atheism's leading representative in the public arena. Yet a close reading of his works—which I try to provide in my forthcoming book *Dawkins' God: Genes, Memes and the Meaning of Life*—suggests that his arguments rest more on fuzzy logic and aggressive rhetoric than on serious evidence-based argument. As America's leading evolutionary biologist, the late Stephen Jay Gould, insisted, the natural sciences simply cannot adjudicate on the God question. If the sciences are used to defend either atheism or religious beliefs, they are misused.

Atheism Has Become a Kind of Tyranny

Yet atheism has not simply run out of intellectual steam. Its moral credentials are now severely tarnished. Once, it was possible to argue that religion alone was the source of the world's evils. Look at the record of violence of the Spanish Inquisition (interestingly, recent research has challenged this historical stereotype). Or the oppression of the French people in the 1780s under the Roman Catholic Church and the Bourbon monarchy. The list could be extended endlessly to make the same powerful moral point: wherever religion exercises power, it oppresses and corrupts, using violence to enforce its own beliefs and agendas. Atheism argued that it abolished this tyranny by getting rid of what ultimately caused it—faith in God.

Yet that argument now seems tired, stale and unconvincing. It was credible in the 19th century precisely because atheism had never enjoyed the power and influence once exercised by religion. But all that has changed. Atheism's innocence has now evaporated. In the 20th century, atheism managed to grasp the power that had hitherto eluded it. And it proved just as fallible, just as corrupt and just as oppressive as anything that had gone before it. [Joseph] Stalin's death squads were just as murderous as their religious antecedents. Those

Atheism Does Not Offer Compassion or Demand Accountability

Secularism has so little to say about human suffering. It is simply not satisfying to those who feel pain at life's extremities. Secular humanism lacks the resources to explain why self-sacrifice has meaning. Moreover, it offers little in the way of remedy to those who have done evil and now repent of it. Such persons cannot be fooled by therapy; they know exactly what they did and they know that they chose deliberately to do it. They are not seeking understanding but rather the erasure of real guilt for the real evils they have committed.

Michael Novak, "Remembering the Secular Age,"
First Things, *June-July 2007, p. 35.*

who dreamed of freedom in the new atheist paradise often found themselves counting trees in Siberia, or confined to the gulags—and they were the fortunate ones.

Like many back in the late 1960s, I was quite unaware of the darker side of atheism, as practised in the Soviet Union. I had assumed that religion would die away naturally, in the face of the compelling intellectual arguments and moral vision offered by atheism. I failed to ask what might happen if people did not want to have their faith eliminated. A desire to eliminate belief in God at the intellectual or cultural level has the most unfortunate tendency to encourage others to do this at the physical level. [Vladimir] Lenin, frustrated by the Russian people's obstinate refusal to espouse atheism voluntarily and naturally after the Russian Revolution, enforced it, arguing in a famous letter of March 1922 that the 'protracted use of brutality' was the necessary means of achieving this goal.

Some of the greatest atrocities of the 20th century were committed by regimes which espoused atheism, often with a fanaticism that some naive Western atheists seem to think is reserved only for religious people. As [British author] Martin Amis stressed in *Koba the Dread*, we now know what really happened under Stalin, even if it was unfashionable to talk about this in progressive circles in the West until the 1990s. The firing squads that Stalin sent to liquidate the Buddhist monks of Mongolia gained at least something of their fanaticism and hatred of religion from those who told them that religion generated fanaticism and hatred.

The real truth here seems to be that identified by [German philosopher Friedrich] Nietzsche at the end of the 19th century—that there is something about human nature which makes it capable of being inspired by what it believes to be right to do both wonderful and appalling things. Neither atheism nor religion may be at fault—it might be some deeply troubling flaw in human nature itself. It is an uncomfortable thought, but one that demands careful reflection.

Only Religion Captures the Hearts and Minds of the People

A further problem for atheism is that its appeal seems to be determined by its social context, not intrinsic to its ideas. Where religion is seen to oppress, confine, deprive and limit, atheism may well be seen to offer humanity a larger vision of freedom. But where religion anchors itself in the hearts and minds of ordinary people, is sensitive to their needs and concerns, and offers them a better future, the atheist critique is unpersuasive. In the past, atheism offered a vision which captured the imagination of Western Europe. We all need to dream, to imagine a better existence—and atheism empowered people to overthrow the past, and create a brave new world.

The appeal of atheism as a public philosophy came to an undistinguished end in 1989 with the collapse of the Berlin Wall. Atheism, once seen as a liberator, was now cordially loathed as an oppressor. The beliefs were pretty much the same as before; their appeal, however, was very different. As the Soviet empire crumbled at a dizzying rate in the 1990s, those who had once been 'liberated' from God rushed to embrace him once more. Islam is resurgent in central Soviet Asia, and Orthodoxy in Russia itself. Harsh and bitter memories of state-enforced atheism linger throughout Eastern Europe, with major implications for the religious and cultural future of the European Union as former Soviet bloc nations achieve membership.

Where people enjoy their religion, seeing it as something life-enhancing and identity-giving, they are going to find atheism unattractive. The recent surge of evidence-based studies demonstrating the positive impact of religion on human well-being has yet to be assimilated by atheist writers. It is only where religion is seen as the enemy that atheism's demands for its elimination will be taken seriously. Atheism's problem is that its own baleful legacy in the former Soviet Union has led many to view it as the enemy, and religion as its antidote. In Eastern Europe, atheism is widely seen as politically discredited and imaginatively exhausted.

But what of Western Europe, which has known state Churches and a religious establishment, but never the state atheism that casts such a dark shadow over its future in the East? Surely, atheism can hope for greater things here? The West, having been spared first-hand experience of atheism as the authoritarian (anti)religion of the establishment, still has some vague, lingering memories of a religious past that atheism could build on. Yet there are real problems here. For a new challenge to atheism has arisen within the West, which atheist writers have been slow to recognise and reluctant to engage—postmodernism.

Atheists Seem Unable to Change with the Times

Historians of ideas often note that atheism is the ideal religion of modernity—the cultural period ushered in by the Enlightenment. But that had been displaced by postmodernity, which rejects precisely those aspects of modernity that made atheism the obvious choice as the preferred modern religion. Postmodernity has thus spawned post-atheism. Yet atheism seems to be turning a blind eye to this massive cultural shift, and the implications for the future of its faith.

In marked contrast, gallons of ink have been spilled and immense intellectual energy expended by Christian writers in identifying and meeting the challenges of postmodernism. Two are of particular relevance here. First, in general terms, postmodernism is intensely suspicious of totalizing worldviews, which claim to offer a global view of reality. Christian apologists have realised that there is a real challenge here. If Christianity claims to be right where others are wrong, it has to make this credible to a culture which is strongly resistant to any such claims to be telling the whole truth. Second, again in general terms, postmodernity regards purely materialist approaches to reality as inadequate, and has a genuine interest in recovering 'the spiritual dimension to life'. For Christian apologists, this is a problem, as this new interest in spirituality has no necessary connection with organised religion of any kind, let alone Christianity. How can the Churches connect with such aspirations?

Atheism has been slow, even reluctant, to engage with either of these developments, tending to dismiss them as irrational and superstitious (Richard Dawkins is a case in point). Yet it is easy to see why the rise of postmodernity poses a significantly greater threat to atheism than to Christianity. Atheism offers precisely the kind of 'meta-narrative' that postmodern thinkers hold to lead to intolerance and oppression. Its uncompromising and definitive denial of God is now seen as arrogant and repressive, rather than as principled and moral.

The postmodern interest in spirituality is much more troubling for atheism than for Christianity. For the Christian, the problem is how to relate or convert an interest in spirituality to the Church or to Jesus Christ. But at least it points in the right direction. For the atheist, it represents a quasi-superstitious reintroduction of spiritual ideas, leading post-modernity backwards into religious beliefs that atheism thought it had exorcised. Atheism seems curiously disconnected from this shift in cultural mood. It seems that atheists are greying, inhabiting a dying modern world, while around them a new interest in the forbidden fruit of the spiritual realm is gaining the upper hand, above all among young people. Consider the immense popularity of the Alpha course, whose advertisements may be seen on London buses, and whose adherents are now said to number some 60 million worldwide; or the expansion of Pentecostalism, now attracting half a billion global followers. Even 9/11 [2001, terrorist attacks on America], a religiously motivated assault, did not prompt an atheist backlash, but an upsurge in interest in Islam. What, I wonder, are the implications of such developments for the future of atheism in the West?

I see no reason why atheism cannot regain some of its lost ground—but not as a public philosophy, commanding wide assent and demanding privileged access to the corridors of power. It will do so as a private belief system, respectful of the beliefs of others. Instead of exulting in disrespect and contempt for religious belief, atheism will see itself as one option among many, entitled to the same respect that it accords others. The most significant, dynamic and interesting critic of Western Christianity is no longer atheism, but a religious alternative, offering a rival vision of God—Islam. This is not what the atheist visionaries of the past wanted, but it seems to be the way things are going.

> *"Intelligent design theory is not based on the Bible or any other scripture. It is not creationism in disguise, as opponents of intelligent design misleadingly claim. Intelligent design accepts evolution as a fact."*

Science and Religion Can Coexist

Stafford Betty

In the following viewpoint, Stafford Betty contends that both intelligent design and Darwinian evolution should be taught in schools. He maintains that evolution is not only a secular belief and that supporters of Darwinian evolution are unrealistic because they cannot accept that only the guiding hand of God could have directed the path of evolution. Stafford Betty is a professor of religious studies at California State University at Bakersfield.

As you read, consider the following questions:

1. According to Stafford Betty, why is Darwinism "not the same thing as evolution"?

2. In Betty's opinion, how does a wing evolving from a dinosaur's forearm show a flaw in Darwinian evolution?

3. According to the author, what does "guided evolution" mean?

Although a frequent critic of President [George W.] Bush, I think he was correct to say that intelligent design theory deserves a mention in science classrooms alongside Darwinian evolution.

Intelligent design theory is not based on the Bible or any other scripture. It is not creationism in disguise, as opponents of intelligent design misleadingly claim. Intelligent design accepts evolution as a fact. It accepts an ancient earth (4.6 billion years) and a still more ancient universe (13.7 billion years). It accepts all the findings of responsible science. But it does not accept Darwinism.

Darwinism is not the same thing as evolution. It is a particular theory of how evolution occurred. According to Darwinism, the entire process was unguided and happened "naturally." Intelligent design theorists contest this claim. They call into question Darwinian evolution's cardinal doctrine, natural selection. Proponents of natural selection claim that the process by which more complex organisms arise from less complex ones is not guided by any intelligence. Proponents of intelligent design say it is.

Supporters of intelligent design hold that Darwinian evolution is not good science. Here is why:

According to the tenets of Darwinian evolution, a genetic accident within a member of a species sometimes (actually very rarely) has a beneficial effect on the species. Consider archaeopteryx, the transitional form between dinosaur and bird that Darwinian evolution holds is the ancestor of birds as we know them. A long series of genetic accidents gradually turns the dinosaur's forearm into a feathery appendage (wing) that enables the archaeopteryx to better flee its enemy by soaring above the ground. And that advantage gives it a much better chance of surviving. Thus birds evolve from dinosaurs, according to standard Darwinian teaching. In a similar manner every species has evolved. All is explained by a long series of lucky genetic accidents, the survival of the fittest, and a steady march forward across hundreds of millions of years from blue-green algae to Mother Teresa.

A Flaw of the Darwinian Theory

The theory sounds great, as no doubt you were told in your high school biology class. But it has one potentially fatal flaw. Let's get back to the example of the feathery appendage. There is no evidence that the wing evolved in one fell swoop. Darwinians grant that it took a whole series of genetic accidents spanning millions of years for the wing to fully evolve. At first there was just some extra fluff on the dinosaur's forearms. Then a little more. Then still more. Then something that resembled feathers. Then more feathers. And finally two wings that enabled the first proto-bird to rise off the ground.

Do you begin to see the problem? What survival advantage did the first genetic accident resulting in a little extra fluff on its forearms give the dinosaur? Or even the 20th fortuitous accident resulting in something genuinely feathery? None that intelligent design can see, because the dinosaur still can't fly. So what would push the dinosaur along such a line of evolutionary development? Nothing that intelligent design can see unless there was some kind of intelligence guiding the evolution. Some kind of intelligence that saw in advance that this long and gradual process would result in that marvelous life form we refer to as a bird. Some kind of intelligence that wanted birds inhabiting our earth and knew how to bring it about—by a guided evolution.

There are thousands of instances like this that resist explanation via Darwinian evolution. Try explaining, for example, what the survival value was for us when our ancestors lost

Religion and Science Are Both Powerful Forces

Can science and religion learn to live with each other? The answer is that they had better or we will all suffer the consequences. Even those who do not participate in either of them will concede that religion and science are two of our most powerful and pervasive influences. Both have been major forces in the development of Western civilization. Of the two, only religion addresses the existential questions: Why am I here? What is expected of me, and by whom? Is there a layer of reality beyond the visible? Is there any continuity after death? Science, meanwhile, investigates the tangible world of experience. It is responsible for most of our technology and thus for much of our prosperity.

Murray Peshkin, "Why We Can't Dilute Darwin,"
Chicago Tribune, *February 12, 2006, p. 17.*

their tails and fur. We find hairy apes at the equator and some of the least hairy humans on the planet inside the Arctic Circle. Natural selection? This is just one of many anomalies that leave me scratching my head and looking for some other explanation.

Opponents of intelligent design label this "other explanation" unscientific. Is it? Supporters of intelligent design claim that evolution was guided; supporters of Darwinian evolution claim it wasn't. Is it really unscientific to claim that an unseen intelligence guided the evolution? I don't see why. Human intelligence is unseen. But we all know that it's behind our homes and our cities. To acknowledge that in almost every case intelligent choices create order isn't unscientific.

Is it unscientific to point out the weakness in Darwinian evolution? Leading theorists of intelligent design such as Michael Behe and William Dembski think it's good science. They single out organs, like the human eye, or even highly complex molecules and show that they are "irreducibly complex"—that is, the supposed transitional forms leading to but falling well short of them wouldn't have been any more fit to survive than their starting point. So how could the end product have evolved? Unless, of course, it was all along on the radarscope of an unseen, intelligence guiding the evolution to its target, as most Catholics believe.

The argument presented here is not based on the Bible. True, many Bible-based Christians have championed it. It is, after all, much more compatible with their beliefs than Darwinian evolution, for there is nothing to rule out the possibility that the unseen intelligence is much more than a designer. But what one's faith adds to the designer does not affect the validity of the argument for intelligent design.

I will conclude by quoting from Einstein. "You will hardly find one among the profounder sort of scientific minds without a peculiar religious feeling of his own. . . . His religious feeling takes the form of a rapturous amazement at the harmony of natural law, which reveals an intelligence of such superiority that, compared with it, all the systematic thinking and acting of human beings is an utterly insignificant reflection."

The "intelligence" Einstein refers to is the same sort of intelligence intelligent design points to. Would anyone want to claim that Einstein's conclusions are unscientific or faith-based or his reasoning invalid? Or that his views are inappropriate for a science classroom?

> *"The war of religion against science has merely shifted to new battlegrounds, but it still rages on."*

Science and Religion Cannot Coexist

Keith Lockitch

In the following viewpoint, Keith Lockitch argues that any apparent harmony between science and religion is false. He cites the calendar definition of Easter as one example in a long history of conflict between science and religion. He claims that the conflict is now waged over new ideas, such as the age of the earth, but is much the same as it was many years ago. Lockitch, who has a PhD in physics, is a resident fellow at the Ayn Rand Institute and focuses on science and environmentalism.

As you read, consider the following questions:

1. What rule defines the day that Easter falls on each year?
2. Who was Nicolas Copernicus?
3. According to Keith Lockitch, why was the Church's persecution of Galileo hypocritical?

In 1582 Pope Gregory XIII established our modern calendar and fixed the rules determining the date of Easter. This year [2008] Easter falls on March 23, but from year to year it can shift by as much as a month on the Gregorian calendar.

Finding Easter's date for a given year requires a surprising degree of scientific acumen. The last things one might expect to see in, say, the Book of Common Prayer are tables of numbers and rules for mathematical calculations—but there they are, nevertheless.

At first glance, this seems to exemplify a kind of harmony between religion and science, a peaceful concord between faith and reason. Indeed, a variety of public figures—from prominent scientists to the Pope—have promoted the view that science and religion are not adversaries but complementary and mutually supporting fields. "Truth cannot contradict truth," they declare, implying that the truths discovered by reasoning from sensory evidence cannot clash with the "truths" of religious dogma.

A closer look, however, reveals the long history of the hostility of faith towards reason—which continues to this day. Violent clashes between the two are not only possible but unavoidable, and the notion that religion can coexist on friendly terms with science and reason is false.

Easter and the Earth's Orbit

For reasons both biblical and astronomical, Easter is defined as the first Sunday after the first full moon on or after the vernal equinox (the first day of spring). To get his calendar rules right, Pope Gregory had to rely on some of the best astronomers and mathematicians of his day. Ironically, one of these was Nicolas Copernicus, whose sun-centered astronomy engendered one of history's most famous clashes between science and religion.

A faithful canon of the Catholic Church, Copernicus supported the calendar project happily. His scientific work was partly motivated by the goal of predicting more accurately the

Science Explains What Religion Cannot

Real evolution isn't random; it doesn't say man came from monkeys. Those claims are made up by critics to get people riled up—paving the way for pleasing alternatives like intelligent design.

Real evolutionary theory explains how life forms change across generations by passing on helpful traits to their offspring; a process that, after millions of years, gradually transforms one species into another. This does not happen randomly but through nature's tendency to reward the most successful organisms and to kill the rest.

Edward Humes, "Unintelligent Designs on Darwin,"
Los Angeles Times, *February 12, 2007, p. A19.*

first day of spring and the subsequent full moon. He modestly expressed the hope that by facilitating the calculation of Easter his labors would "contribute somewhat even to the Commonwealth of the Church."

At first Copernicus's work was warmly accepted by Church officials—but only because they didn't take it seriously. Sixteenth century common sense held that the Sun orbits the Earth, which is motionless at the center of the universe. More important, Church scholars held that the true structure of the world is established not by science but by official interpretation of Scripture. Hence, they regarded the motion of the Earth as nothing more than a convenient mathematical assumption—an idea justified solely by its utility in making astronomical predictions. Thinking they could evade a clash between reason and revelation, they denied the reality of the Earth's motion but used the Copernican theory nonetheless.

This contradiction became inescapable decades after the Gregorian reform when Galileo removed the objections from common sense by explaining the physics of the moving Earth. But the objections from faith proved more intractable. Galileo's outspoken defense of the Earth's motion as a serious physical idea forced Church leaders to take a stand—and when they got off the fence, they came down firmly against science. That the Church persecuted Galileo for defending Copernican theory is well-known. Less frequently acknowledged is the utter hypocrisy of that act: *the Church persecuted Galileo for defending the very ideas on which its Easter reform depended.*

In 1992 Pope John Paul II grudgingly admitted—350 years too late—that his predecessors had been wrong. He called the Church's persecution of Galileo a "sad misunderstanding" that "now belongs to the past."

But does it?

The Battle Rages On

Although few would now declare the Earth the motionless center of the universe, it is not difficult to find those who claim it to be 6,000 years old and deny the long, slow evolution of its species. More alarming is that the same Dark Ages mentality that dragged Galileo before the Inquisition now seeks to prohibit entire fields of scientific research, such as therapeutic cloning. The war of religion against science has merely shifted to new battlegrounds, but it still rages on.

Religion's alleged harmony with science is a fraudulent masquerade, extending only insofar as religious dogmas are not called into question. True defenders of science must be committed to reason as an absolute principle—following facts wherever they lead and bowing to no authorities but logic and reality. And they must understand that the servile obedience demanded by faith is wholly incompatible with science—and with the rational thinking on which all human progress and prosperity depends.

"Many atheist sects are experimenting with building new, human-centered quasi-religious organizations. . . . They aim to remove God from the church, while leaving the church, at least large parts of it, standing."

Atheists Disagree About Incorporating Religious Customs and Traditions into Atheism

Sean McManus

In the following viewpoint, Sean McManus reports that the number of Americans who have no religious affiliation has grown in recent years. As this number has increased, so, too, have calls from some in the atheist movement for the need to emphasize the positive aspects of secularism, including establishing community centers that are similar to churches. This is opposed by some atheists who believe that creating such centers would serve only to blur the distinction between religion and atheism. Sean McManus is a writer who contributes to New York *magazine.*

As you read, consider the following questions:

1. According to a Pew Forum on Religion & Public Life survey, what percentage of Americans have no religious affiliation?

2. What are the names of the four men who write about the New Atheism?

3. What is the name of the founder of American Atheists?

It seems unlikely that many of the 850 or so people at the Society for Ethical Culture on a recent Saturday night believed that God was still extant. But evolutionary biologist Richard Dawkins, author of *The God Delusion* and possibly the most famous atheist in the world, was not taking any chances. He gave a PowerPoint presentation driving home that religion does not meet any of the standards of basic scientific inquiry, before casually flicking away a few of His last crutches. Doesn't God provide people some solace? asked an audience member. "Isn't that a little childish?" Dawkins replied. "Just because something is comforting doesn't mean it's true." Then someone asked about death, and Dawkins quoted Mark Twain: "I do not fear death. I had been dead for billions and billions of years before I was born." The room erupted in loud applause. God had definitely left the building—if he were ever here at all. Dawkins and his colleagues had helped to produce a kind of atheist big bang, a new beginning. But what kind of new structures might evolve?

The Society for Ethical Culture was formed in 1877, eighteen years after Charles Darwin published *On the Origin of Species* and made the religious universe wobble on its axis. But godlessness can be a little scary, even for an atheist. Ethical Culture's imposing 1910 edifice on Central Park speaks to its patrons' wealth, as well as their concern that society might fall apart if it didn't have a church. But for all the grandeur of its secular cathedral, Ethical Culture peaked at maybe 6,000 members, with only about 3,000 today.

More People Do Not Believe in God

Now, once again, nonbelievers have a fresh sense of mission. The fastest-growing faith in the country is no faith at all. The Pew Forum on Religion & Public Life released the results of its "Religious Landscape" survey in February [2008] and found that 16 percent of Americans have no religious affiliation. The number is even greater among young people: 25 percent of 18- to 29-year-olds now identify with no religion, up from 11 percent in a similar survey in 1986. For most of its modern history, atheism has existed as a kind of civil-rights movement. Groups like American Atheists have functioned primarily as litigants in the fight for church-state separation, not as atheist social clubs. "Atheists are self-reliant, self-sufficient, independent people who don't feel like they need an organization," says Ellen Johnson, president of American Atheists for the past thirteen years. "They're so independent that if they want to get involved, they usually don't join an organization—they start their own."

The quartet of best-selling authors who have emerged to write the gospel of New Atheism—Sam Harris, Daniel Dennett, Christopher Hitchens, and Dawkins (the Four Horsemen, as they are now known)—has succeeded in mainstreaming atheism in a nation that is still overwhelmingly religious and, in the process, catalyzed a reexamination of atheistic raison d'être [reasons for existence]. But for some atheist foot soldiers, this current groundswell is just a consciousness-raising stop on the evolutionary train, the atheist equivalent of the Stonewall riots. For these people, the Four Horsemen have only started the journey. Atheism's great awakening is in need of a doctrine. "People perceive us as only rejecting things," says Ken Bronstein, the president of a local group called New York City Atheists. "Everybody wants to know, 'Okay, you're an atheist, now what?'"

So some atheists are taking seriously the idea that atheism needs to stand for things, like evolution and ethics, not just against things, like God. The most successful movements in history, after all—Christianity, Islam, Hinduism, etc.—all have creeds, cathedrals, schools, hierarchies, rituals, money, clerics, and some version of a heavenly afterlife. Churches fill needs, goes the argument—they inculcate ethics, give meaning, build communities. "Science and reason are important," says Greg Epstein, the humanist chaplain of Harvard University. "But science and reason won't visit you in the hospital."

Following the Lead of Churches

Many atheist sects are experimenting with building new, human-centered quasi-religious organizations, much like Ethical Culture. They aim to remove God from the church, while leaving the church, at least large parts of it, standing. But this impulse is fueling a growing schism among atheists. Many of them see churches as part of the problem. They want to throw out the baby *and* the bathwater—or at least they don't see the need for the bathwater once the baby is gone.

On a recent chilly Friday night, a few dozen members of the City Congregation for Humanistic Judaism were gathered downstairs at the Village Community School on West 10th Street for Shabbat. For them, this is a monthly ritual that includes lighting candles and singing Jewish songs that have been carefully excised of a deity. "Where is my light?" asks the song "Ayfo Oree." "My light is in me." According to the congregation's leader, the humanist rabbi Peter Schweitzer, who wrote much of the secular Shabbat service, as well as the lyrics and verse for the congregation's life-cycle events like weddings, funerals, and bar and bat mitzvahs, Judaism is mostly a culture—religion is just one component. So he simply takes a red pen to the God parts. "We offer a different door in," says Schweitzer. "One that doesn't ask you to compromise your lack of beliefs."

Schweitzer tells me that Humanistic Judaism was founded in the early sixties by a former Reform rabbi from Michigan named Sherwin Wine. Wine, Schweitzer explains, coined the term *ignostic*—you're never going to know what God is, so why waste your time worrying about it? "God is a construct of the mind," he says. "Maybe you get there. Maybe you don't."

Schweitzer sees Humanistic Judaism as an obvious extension of a North American Jewry that is already highly secular—one that for decades has made "the deli a more significant cultural force than the synagogue." Many secular Jews continue to feel a strong connection to their cultural roots. "Jews need a place to go, especially during high holidays, where they don't have to check reason at the door," he says. "This is honest religion. A real gift."

After Shabbat, I talked to a retired philosophy professor, Marvin Kohl, an expert on Bertrand Russell, who admitted, reluctantly, that he believes in God. "I like the intellectual side," he says of the meetings. Before the night was over, a speaker from Jews for Racial and Economic Justice gave a talk about affordable housing. Then Schweitzer reminded the congregation that it needs new office space. There aren't enough members to afford a synagogue.

Atheist orthodoxy for the most part has been an oxymoron, partly because atheist leaders have tended toward a certain eccentricity. Before the Four Horsemen arrived, the face of atheism in this country belonged to Madalyn Murray O'Hair—"Mad Madalyn"—the pugnacious founder of American Atheists who disowned her son when he became a Baptist preacher and publicly pronounced it a "postnatal abortion." Angry and overweight, she was the muse of daytime-talk-show host Phil Donahue and a speechwriter for Larry Flynt. In 1964, *Life* magazine crowned her "the most hated woman in America." O'Hair was murdered and dismembered, allegedly by her office manager, David Roland Waters, in 1995, but this wasn't discovered until six years later, prompting speculation in the meantime that she had fled to the South Pacific with piles of atheist loot. January 2001 signaled a low point in

Atheism Needs to Offer the Comfort That Religion Provides

It is true that in times of crisis, we feel compelled to fall back on those systems of belief with the deepest roots, and religion certainly has a long history. This is the reason many believe the idea that "there are no atheists in foxholes." What they may fail to realize is that the same impulse to fall back on various roots does not always mean that individuals will adopt a religious stance. We also have a long history of skepticism, and mistrust in the abuses of power. If the traditions of science, skepticism, and free thought are to survive any assault, its roots must be as deep as any religion. Individuals will need to feel the same sense of community and support from atheism as they do in their respective faiths. How else can we hope for individuals to remove their dependence on superstition to provide comfort and familiarity?

Jacob Fortin, "Is Atheism a Religion?"
The Good Atheist, *June 18, 2007. http://thegoodatheist.net.*

contemporary atheist history. The same month Waters led police to the remains of the woman who successfully fought to end prayer in public schools, a Pew survey found that only 19 percent of Americans thought schools should avoid prayer or similar reflection.

Do Atheists Need a Church?

Orthodox or not, for many traditional atheists, the word *church* is taboo, even if God is definitely not in residence. When Tim Gorski, a Texas physician, approached Paul Kurtz, an influential atheist who now chairs the Center for Inquiry, an atheist think tank, about his plans to start the North Texas Church of Freethought in the nineties, Kurtz discouraged him, on the grounds that atheists don't need church. And about ten years ago, American Atheists turned down Gorski's bid to sign on to an atheist advertisement published in *USA Today*. "Individuals and organizations could put their names on the ad. Churches could not," Ellen Johnson wrote me in an e-mail, while insisting that American Atheism's "eleventh commandment" is to never criticize or rebuke kindred organizations. "Since they were technically a church, we said no."

Gorski believes that a church is not necessarily God's house. It belongs, first, to the people. Many atheists, he says, misunderstand why people go to church in the first place. "It isn't the specific doctrines," he says. "[Church] binds people together and relates them to one another and gives them each a personal, private, and, of course, quite subjective understanding of themselves and their world."

"Every service is different," says Gorski. "For example, we created a serial feature called 'Moment of Science,' where we look at something recent or not so recent but something from science that informs our everyday experience. Economists tell us that if our neighbors live in nicer houses, we're unhappy. We share this with members, so that next time they're unhappy, they can think about why and hopefully change that."

Atheism's bitterest schisms, no surprise, were often formed in church. Gorski says he grew up, uneventfully, as a Catholic. "I've got no ax to grind," he says. But at a meeting of the New York City Atheists in January, two former Jehovah's Witnesses recounted a childhood rooted in lies and indoctrination. The young woman, who used a pseudonym for fear of never being able to speak to her parents again, told the audience that her father would hide her *National Geographic*. Ellen Johnson explains it this way: "Our members have left religion and don't want any part of that."

Additionally, many atheists see the challenge of tearing down the pillars of organized religion as far from over—just check the numbers of Americans who don't believe in evolution, they say. And that work—of arguing, of reeducation, of fighting discrimination against nonbelievers—should take precedence over any kind of organization-building.

Atheists Need to Create a Community

As a political strategy, however, that may be shortsighted. Greg Epstein, who like Schweitzer is a student of Humanistic Judaism, is perhaps the most outspoken voice for humanism in the United States and has made waves among atheists by arguing that the militancy of the Four Horsemen could derail an otherwise powerful movement. When I met the 31-year-old Epstein for breakfast in a Soho restaurant last month, he told me he's writing a book called *Good Without God*, due out . . . [in 2009]. "Most nonreligious people are not anti-religious," he says, and he's got the numbers to prove it. Epstein says that when he arrived at Harvard as the assistant humanist chaplain in 2004, there were just a handful of organized nonbelievers and no Web site. Now he has a mailing list of over 3,000 and sponsors popular conferences featuring big-ticket atheists like Salman Rushdie, E.O. Wilson, and Steven Pinker. . . . He's presenting Greg Graffin, co-founder of the punk band Bad Religion, who is also a lecturer on life sciences at UCLA [University of California, Los Angeles], with a lifetime achievement award in humanism. I asked Epstein whether atheists need a church. "I'm saying we need to get organized," he responds. "But what I view as organization still has pleasant disorganization. No humanist will accept authority for authority's sake. It's not in our makeup. If anyone came up and said, 'This is the rule, this is the humanist dogma, and I can tell you based on my authority what the creed is,' we'd throw them out with the trash. There's a difference between building a community and building an atheist regime."

In February [2008], Epstein spoke to members of the Society for Ethical Culture to try to light a fire under an assembly whose numbers have been dwindling for decades. Founded by Felix Adler, the son of a rabbi, to drive social-justice initiatives and promote good without God, Ethical Culture walks like a church and talks like a church—congregants sit in pews, rise to sing hymns, and pass around a collection plate. But at one of their Sunday-morning meetings in January, their Senior Leader, in a very unchurchlike fashion, cited agnosticism as the only intellectually defensible religious position. More to the point, Epstein is eyeing the group's building as a prototype for the church of New Humanism. Modeled on a Greco-Roman coliseum, Ethical Culture has semi-circular pews to promote conversation and a low stage designed to minimize the distance between leader and congregation. "I want to build big, beautiful buildings like Ethical Culture in every big city in America," says Epstein. Unfortunately, his organization only brings in $200,000 a year. And while that's up from $28,000 four years ago, it's not enough to build a New Humanist church in Cambridge, Massachusetts, let alone Central Park West.

The Four Horsemen haven't completely turned their back on the movement they've helped to ignite. In addition to working on a children's book about evolution to be published in 2009, the bicentennial of Darwin's birth, Richard Dawkins has launched his Web-based campaign to encourage atheists to come out of the closet. In lieu of a rainbow flag, he sells T-shirts with the scarlet letter *A*. Sam Harris, who says playing the victim is the wrong approach, is starting something called the Reason Project, bringing entertainers into the movement to further atheism's passage into the mainstream. Celebrity atheists like Bill Maher, Ian McKellen, and Julia Sweeney, whose one-woman show *Letting Go of God* is a big hit at atheist conferences, have been vital to the renewed energy behind the movement. "Nobody is satisfied with the profusion of groups and meetings," says Harris. "My starting yet another organization is unhelpful on that front."

A Somewhat Disconnected Perspective

At this point, the movement can't even agree on a name. Christopher Hitchens, author of *God Is Not Great*, prefers the term *anti-theist* because he's entertained the possibility that God exists and finds the prospect frightening, the spiritual equivalent of living in North Korea. Daniel Dennett continues to promote the term *bright*, which, he has said, is "modeled very deliberately and very consciously on the homosexual adoption of the word *gay*." (In the first chapter of *God Is Not Great*, Hitchens dismisses the term as conceited.) And Sam Harris, brash young scientist that he is, triggered a minor revolt last fall [2007] at the Atheist Alliance International Conference in Crystal City, Virginia, when he lashed out against the term *atheist*, disparaging those who identify with a negation. "It reverberated in atheist circles as a sacrilege," Harris told me. "But what's worse is adopting language that was placed on us by religious people. We don't feel the need to brand ourselves non-astrologers or non-racists."

Dennett sees value in atheism's great awakening, in the energy and money that come from organizing, but he counsels caution. "The last thing atheists want to see is their rational set of ideas yoked up with the trappings of a religion," he says. "We think we can do without that." Even Richard Dawkins is not one to reject certain memes based on their churchly pedigree. He calls himself a "cultural Christian," admitting that he likes to sing Christmas carols as much as the next guy. But there's a limit to his tolerance of religion. He can see the tactical virtues of making temporary alliances with religion—to "hold hands with religious people" when it comes to making the case for important causes like teaching evolution in the classroom. But there are definite limits. "In the larger war against supernaturalism, frankly, it doesn't help to fraternize with the enemy," he says.

Periodical Bibliography

The following articles have been selected to supplement the diverse views presented in this chapter.

Rich Barlow   "Fostering Community in Nontheism," *Boston Globe*, April 19, 2008.

Sam Blumenfeld   "Intelligent by Design," *Practical Homeschooling*, July-August 2005.

Brian P. Brennan   "Atheism Is Its Own Belief System," *National Catholic Reporter*, March 25, 2005.

Theodore Dalrymple   "Tolerance, if Not Respect," *National Review*, March 13, 2006.

Cornelia Dean   "Faith, Reason, God and Other Imponderables," *New York Times*, July 25, 2006.

George Felis   "Come Out, Come Out, Wherever You Are," March 2007. http://thenewhumanist.com.

John F. Haught   "True Believers: Have the New Atheists Adopted a Faith of Their Own?" *America*, May 5, 2008.

David Masci   "The 'Evidence for Belief': An Interview with Francis Collins," April 17, 2008. www.pewforum.org.

Matthew C. Nisbet and Chris Mooney   "Thanks for the Facts: Now Sell Them," *Washington Post*, April 15, 2007.

Phyllis Schlafly   "Criticism of Evolution Can't Be Silenced," *Human Events*, August 21, 2006.

Herb Silverman   "Compete or Cooperate? Endorse, Ignore or Oppose?" *The Humanist*, September-October 2007.

For Further Discussion

Chapter 1

1. After reading the viewpoints in this chapter on the prevalence of atheism in society, do you believe that atheists are outsiders in the United States? Explain your reasoning and use quotes from the viewpoints to support your thinking.

2. Barbara Ehrenreich contends that people who believe in God should question their belief after the devastation of the tsunami that took place on December 26, 2004. In the opposing viewpoint, Roger Scruton argues that there is nothing irrational about believing that God exists because prayer and faith help us to find answers to our questions about life, even when faced with devastating situations. Do you agree or disagree with Ehrenreich, Scruton, or both? Use information from Ehrenreich's and Scruton's articles to support your statements.

Chapter 2

1. James Haught argues that atheism benefits society because it promotes honesty and urges people to be skeptical of religious claims for which there is no evidence. Dinesh D'Souza maintains that atheism harms society because many millions of people have been killed in attempting to rid the world of religion. Which argument do you think makes a stronger case? Use quotes from the viewpoints to support your view.

2. In his viewpoint arguing that atheism teaches morality and ethics, Paul Kurtz uses the phrase "Gott mit uns" ("God is with us") negatively to assert that religious morality expects strict adherence to religious beliefs and doesn't allow for differing opinions. In the opposing view-

point, Stephen Pope might use the same phrase more positively by maintaining that belief in God motivates people to be more concerned for and kind toward others. For which argument do you think the phrase "Gott mit uns" is more effective? Why or why not?

Chapter 3

1. After evaluating the two viewpoints on the separation of church and state, decide what you think the Founding Fathers really intended when they wrote the Constitution. Use information from Marci Hamilton's and Warner Todd Huston's viewpoints to support your answer.

2. In Patton Dodd's interview with Stephen Prothero, Prothero maintains that instructors can teach students about religion without preaching their personal beliefs. In the opposing viewpoint, Rob Boston uses Matthew LaClair's story to argue that religion should not be taught in public schools because it cannot be taught objectively. Do you think that religion can be taught objectively in school? Why or why not?

Chapter 4

1. Keith Lockitch argues that science and religion cannot be reconciled because science offers evidence while religion offers only belief in God. Stafford Betty maintains that the two can coexist because intelligent design accepts evolution but contends that evolution has been directed by God. Which argument do you think is more persuasive? Why?

2. After reading Sean McManus's viewpoint on whether or not atheism has become a religion, do you believe that atheism should adopt certain religious traditions in order to expand its appeal? Do you believe that atheism loses its central difference from religion by doing so? Why or why not?

Organizations to Contact

The editors have compiled the following list of organizations concerned with the issues debated in this book. The descriptions are derived from materials provided by the organizations. All have publications or information available for interested readers. The list was compiled on the date of publication of the present volume; the information provided here may change. Be aware that many organizations take several weeks or longer to respond to inquiries, so allow as much time as possible.

American Atheists
PO Box 5733, Parsippany, NJ   07054
(908) 276-7300
e-mail: info@atheists.org
Web site: www.atheists.org

Founded by Madalyn Murray O'Hair in 1963, American Atheists is an organization devoted to ensuring that complete separation of church and state is preserved. The group is dedicated to promoting secularism in all facets of society. Its publications include *American Atheist Magazine*.

American Center for Law & Justice (ACLJ)
PO Box 90555, Washington, DC   20090-0555
(800) 296-4529
Web site: www.aclj.org

The mission of the American Center for Law & Justice (ACLJ) is to ensure that religious liberty and freedom of speech are protected and maintained. ACLJ offers free legal assistance in cases where the group believes religious liberty and freedom of speech are threatened; the center also focuses on national security and pro-life causes. Jay Sekulow, the group's chief counsel, hosts the radio program *Jay Sekulow Live!* and the TV program *ACLJ This Week*, both of which focus on legislative issues and trials dealing with religious rights and freedoms.

American Civil Liberties Union (ACLU)

132 W. Forty-Third Street, New York, NY   10036
(212) 944-9800 • fax: (212) 359-5290
Web site: www.aclu.org

The American Civil Liberties Union (ACLU) is the nation's oldest and largest civil liberties organization. The ACLU provides legal defense, research, and education and publishes the monthly newsletter *Civil Liberties Alert*, as well as pamphlets, books, and position papers.

American Humanist Association (AHA)

1777 T Street NW, Washington, DC   20009-7125
(202) 238-9088 • fax: (202) 238-9003
Web site: www.americanhumanist.org

The American Humanist Association (AHA) is an organization dedicated to promoting humanism in the United States. The group works to educate the public about humanism so that it is more fully understood and accepted. The AHA's publications include *The Humanist* magazine, *Essays in the Philosophy of Humanism* journal, and the *Free Mind* newsletter.

Americans United for Separation of Church and State (AU)

518 C Street NE, Washington, DC   20002
(202) 466-3234 • fax: (202) 466-2587
e-mail: americansunited@au.org
Web site: www.au.org

Americans United for Separation of Church and State (AU) was established in 1947 to defend the right to religious freedom for all Americans. AU works to guarantee that the establishment clause of the First Amendment is maintained. The group publishes *Church & State* magazine, and such brochures as *Science, Religion, and Public Education: An Evolving Controversy* and *America's Legacy of Religious Liberty: Pass It On.*

Answers in Genesis (AiG)
PO Box 510, Hebron, KY   41058
(859) 727-2222
Web site: www.answersingenesis.org

Answers in Genesis (AiG) is a group devoted to helping Christians defend their beliefs by offering responses to questions about the book of Genesis. The organization's mission is to teach others to accept a worldview that is shaped by the Bible, and to show the world that evolution is not true. Publications include *Answers* magazine and the *Answers Research Journal.*

Council for Secular Humanism
PO Box 664, Amherst, NY   14226-0664
(716) 636-7571 • fax: (716) 1733
e-mail: info@secularhumanism.org
Web site: www.secularhumanism.org

The Council for Secular Humanism's mission is to educate the public about secular humanism. The Council believes that science and reason can be used to resolve problems and understand the cosmos. Its publications include the *Free Inquiry* magazine and the *Secular Humanist Bulletin.*

Freedom From Religion Foundation (FFRF)
PO Box 750, Madison, WI   53701
(608) 256-8900 • fax: (608) 256-1116
e-mail: info@ffrf.org
Web site: www.ffrf.org

The mission of the Freedom From Religion Foundation (FFRF), which was founded in 1978, is to promote the idea of the separation of church and state. It opposes prayer in public schools, the use of public funds for religious reasons, and government funding of religious groups. The FFRF's publications include the *Freethought Today* newspaper and such books as *The Born-Skeptic's Guide to the Bible* and *Losing Faith in Faith: From Preacher to Atheist.*

Institute for Creation Research

PO Box 59029, Dallas, TX   75229
(800) 337-0375
Web site: www.icr.org

The Institute for Creation Research is an organization committed to providing information about the accuracy of the Bible. The group offers scientific evidence and research that advance its belief in creationism. The Institute's publications include the monthly magazine *Acts & Facts* and the *Online Defender's Study Bible*.

National Council on Bible Curriculum in Public Schools

PO Box 9743, Greensboro, NC   27429
(877) 662-4253 • fax: (336) 272-7199
Web site: www.bibleinschools.net

The National Council on Bible Curriculum in Public Schools is an organization dedicated to bringing a state-certified Bible course to high school students in the United States. Believing that the teaching of biblical studies is an issue of religious freedom and a First Amendment right, the group contends that the Bible should be studied in school because it is the foundation of American society. The council publishes information about steps to take to implement the program in a school district.

The Rutherford Institute

PO Box 7482, Charlottesville, VA   22906-7482
(434) 978-3888 • fax: (434) 978-1789
e-mail: staff@rutherford.org
Web site: www.rutherford.org

The Rutherford Institute was founded in 1982 and is dedicated to upholding civil and religious liberties by defending such liberties in legal cases and by informing the public about constitutional rights. The institute believes that the right to religious freedom is clearly stated in the First Amendment.

Publications include the *Rutherford Newsletter, Freedom Resource* briefs on such topics as public school religious clubs, and white papers on such topics as freedom of religion.

Bibliography of Books

Brooke Allen   *Moral Minority: Our Skeptical
                     Founding Fathers.* Chicago, IL: Ivan
                     R. Dee, 2006.

Francis Collins   *The Language of God: A Scientist
                     Presents Evidence for Belief.* New York:
                     Free Press, 2006.

Austin Dacey   *The Secular Conscience: Why Belief
                     Belongs in Public Life.* Amherst, NY:
                     Prometheus Books, 2008.

Richard Dawkins   *The God Delusion.* New York:
                     Houghton Mifflin, 2006.

Daniel C. Dennett   *Breaking the Spell: Religion as a
                     Natural Phenomenon.* New York:
                     Penguin Group, 2006.

Bruce J.   *The Battle over School Prayer: How
Dierenfield   Engel v. Vitale Changed America.*
                     Lawrence, KS: University Press of
                     Kansas, 2007.

Dinesh D'Souza   *What's So Great About Christianity.*
                     Washington, DC: Regnery Publishing,
                     2007.

Charles W. Dunn   *The Future of Religion in American
                     Politics (None).* Lexington, KY:
                     University Press of Kentucky, 2008.

Taner Edis   *Science and Nonbelief.* Amherst, NY:
                     Prometheus Books, 2007.

Edward Feser   *The Last Superstition: A Refutation of the New Atheism.* South Bend, IN: St. Augustine's Press, 2008.

Antony Flew   *There Is a God: How the World's Most Notorious Atheist Changed His Mind.* New York: HarperCollins Publishers, 2007.

Becky Garrison   *The New Atheist Crusaders and Their Unholy Grail: The Misguided Quest to Destroy Your Faith.* Nashville, TN: Thomas Nelson, Inc. 2007.

Karl Giberson   *Saving Darwin: How to Be a Christian and Believe in Evolution.* New York: K.S. Giniger Company, 2008.

Deborah B. Haarsma and Loren D. Haarsma   *Origins: A Reformed Look at Creation, Design, and Evolution.* Grand Rapids, MI: Faith Alive Christian Resources, 2007.

Scott Hahn and Benjamin Wiker   *The New Atheism: Dismantling Dawkins' Case Against God.* Steubenville, OH: Emmaus Road Publishing, 2008.

Sam Harris   *The End of Faith: Religion, Terror, and the Future of Reason.* New York: W.W. Norton & Company, 2004.

Sam Harris   *Letter to a Christian Nation.* New York: Knopf, 2006.

Guy P. Harrison   *50 Reasons People Give for Believing in God.* Amherst, NY: Prometheus Books, 2008.

John F. Haught	*God and the New Atheism: A Critical Response to Dawkins, Harris, and Hitchens.* Louisville, KY: Westminster John Knox Press, 2008.
Chris Hedges	*I Don't Believe in Atheists.* New York: Free Press, 2008.
Christopher Hitchens	*God Is Not Great: How Religion Poisons Everything.* New York: Hachette Book Group, 2007.
Christopher Hitchens	*The Portable Atheist: Essential Readings for the Nonbeliever.* Cambridge, MA: Da Capo Press, 2007.
Wilson R. Huhn	*Telling Right from Wrong Without the Help of God.* Durham, NC: Carolina Academic Press, 2008.
Cornelius G. Hunter	*Science's Blind Spot: The Unseen Religion of Scientific Naturalism.* Grand Rapids, MI: Brazos Press, 2007.
Peter Irons	*God on Trial: Landmark Cases From America's Religious Battlefields.* New York: Penguin Group, 2007.
Susan Jacoby	*The Age of American Unreason.* New York: Pantheon Books, 2008.
Timothy Keller	*The Reason for God: Belief in an Age of Skepticism.* New York: Penguin Group, 2008.

Paul Kurtz	*Forbidden Fruit: The Ethics of Humanism*. Amherst, NY: Prometheus Books, 2008.
Paul Kurtz	*What Is Secular Humanism?* Amherst, NY: Prometheus Books, 2007.
John W. Loftus	*Why I Rejected Christianity: A Former Apologist Explains*. Canada: Trafford Publishing, 2006.
Dale McGowan	*Parenting Beyond Belief: On Raising Ethical, Caring Kids Without Religion*. New York: AMACOM, 2007.
Alister McGrath	*The Dawkins Delusion? Atheist Fundamentalism and the Denial of the Divine*. Downers Grove, IL: IVP Books, 2007.
Alister McGrath	*The Twilight of Atheism: The Rise and Fall of Disbelief in the Modern World*. New York: Random House, 2004.
Kenneth R. Miller	*Only a Theory: Evolution and the Battle for America's Soul*. New York: Penguin Group, 2008.
R. Albert Mohler Jr.	*Atheism Remix: A Christian Confronts the New Atheists*. Wheaton, IL: Crossway Books, 2008.
Dean L. Overman	*A Case for the Existence of God*. Lanham, MD: Rowman & Littlefield Publishers, Inc., 2008.
George A. Ricker	*Mere Atheism: No Gods . . . No Problems!* Lincoln, NE: iUniverse, 2007.

David Robertson   *The Dawkins Letters: Challenging Atheist Myths*. Scotland, UK: Christian Focus, 2008.

Tara Ross and Joseph C. Smith Jr.   *Under God: George Washington and the Question of Church and State*. Dallas, TX: Spence Publishing, 2008.

Joan Roughgarden   *Evolution and Christian Faith: Reflections of an Evolutionary Biologist*. Washington, DC: Island Press, 2006.

Victor J. Stenger   *God: The Failed Hypothesis—How Science Shows That God Does Not Exist*. Amherst, NY: Prometheus Books, 2007.

Robert B. Stewart   *The Future of Atheism: Alister McGrath and Daniel Dennett in Dialog*. Minneapolis, MN: Fortress Press, 2008.

Thomas Woodward   *Darwin Strikes Back: Defending the Science of Intelligent Design*. Grand Rapids, MI: Baker Books, 2006.

Ravi K. Zacharias   *The End of Reason: A Response to the New Atheists*. Grand Rapids, MI: Zondervan, 2008.

Index

H